LEGACY OF · THE CAT

by Gloria Stephens

Photographs by Tetsu Yamazaki

Chronicle Books · San Francisco

First published in the United States 1990 by Chronicle Books.

Copyright © 1989 by Yama-Kei Publishers Co., Ltd., photographs copyright © 1989 by Tetsu Yamazaki, text copyright © 1989 by Gloria Stephens. All rights reserved. No part of this book may be reproduced in any form without written permission from the publishers.

First published in Japan by Yama-Kei Publishers Co., Ltd.
Printed in Japan.

Library of Congress Cataloging in Publication Data

Stephens, Gloria.
Legacy of the cat / by Gloria Stephens; photographs by Tetsu Yamazaki.
p.   cm.
Based on: Sekai no neko zukan / Yamazaki Tetsu. 1989.
ISBN 0-87701-695-X (pbk.) : ISBN 0-87701-728-X
1. Cats. 2. Cat breeds. 3. Cats—Pictorial works. I. Yamazaki, Tetsu, 1949–
Sekai no neko zukan. II. Title.
SF442.S744   1990   89-70862
636.8—dc20   CIP

Editing: Deborah Bruce
Book design: Brenda Rae Eno and Yukari Imamura, Tokyo Editorial Center
Cover design: Triad
Typography: Wilsted & Taylor
Distributed in Canada by
Raincoast Books, 112 East
Third Avenue, Vancouver, B.C. V5T 1C8

10 9 8 7 6 5 4 3 2 1

Chronicle Books
275 Fifth Street
San Francisco, California 94103

Contents

Introduction

I have always had a cat, even from the age of one or two, when my mother kept a cat. I had cats when my own children were growing up, and I still have cats. They are a part of my life, of great influence on my living conditions and on what I have grown to be.

When I graduated from high school, I wanted to be an artist or writer. Unfortunately, the university I selected did not have an art school or a school of journalism. My next love was the understanding of life, so I completed degrees in biology and psychology at the University of Mississippi. Even when I lived in the dormitory, I had a young black female cat. That is, until I was reported to the dean of women. I had to find a home for my cat, so I placed her with my future mother-in-law, Estelle Faulkner—Mrs. William Faulkner. Estelle's home, named Roanoak, was on the outskirts of town. There my cat would have the freedom of the house and the nearby woods; I begged Estelle to take her, which she willingly did.

I was to be married in Shanghai, to Estelle's son (by a previous marriage), who was visiting his father in China at that time. This meant I would have to leave my cat at Roanoak for the six months I would be overseas. When I returned from China, Estelle told me that shortly after I left my cat had run away and had not been seen since. I grieved. About a week after my return, while at the Faulkner home, I heard a meowing coming from the woods. I could not believe my eyes as my black cat came running to me. She knew, somehow, that I had returned.

Later, a Siamese kitten was given to me after the black cat died. This was my first purebred cat. I moved to New Orleans, where I went to my first cat show. If I had not gone to that show, my whole life would have been different. I looked at exhibition cats with awe and interest. There was a chocolate point Siamese named GR Ch Makhanda Sprite (I did not know she was the first Cat Fancier's Association Grand Champion Chocolate Point Siamese, and would eventually come to live with me). I reasoned that I had one Siamese: why not two? I made arrangements with the breeder to purchase a show quality chocolate point. After the male kitten, Makhanda Genghi of Mardi Gras, arrived, I entered him in the New Orleans show. He was not well-received by the judges and placed second (there were only two chocolate points). Mind you, I thought he was beautiful and could not understand why the judges didn't place him higher. He was large, had medium-sized ears and was dark for a chocolate; I did not know this was not desirable for a show cat. I showed him again; he received third prize (this time there were three chocolate points).

I took these lower wins as a challenge. I had to have a female cat to produce show quality "chocolates." I saved my money and bought a frost and a chocolate female. After a year of showing them, I received two certificates in the mail; my two cats had been awarded Inter-American Best Chocolate and Best Frost. Shortly after that, Mary Frances Platt, the owner of Makhanda Cattery, gave me a seal point male, Makhanda O Solo Mio of Mardi Gras, who was to father many grand champions. I bred Siamese for about thirteen years. I was able to produce only one chocolate who had type and color. I had lovely frosts, and my cattery became known for them, but never for the chocolates I so desired. I now know that I could have kept on breeding with the Siamese I had and never produced many top chocolates, as there had to be a linkage of type and color.

The step that further changed my life was meeting the members of the Cat Fanciers of New Orleans, who invited me to join their club. In my first year I was made secretary of the club, entry clerk, show treasurer and publicity chairman. How was I to know those jobs were usually filled individually? A strong member of the club at that time was Gladys de Floren, who became my friend, teacher and guide. Later I was elected president and show manager, remaining in those roles for many years.

I named my cattery Mardi Gras and started showing and breeding Siamese in earnest. I became very active as a show clerk and clerked almost every show I attended for the next nine years. During this period I became interested in learning the differences between the breeds and finally had to admit that I wanted to become a judge. I also returned to college and received a degree in fine arts, specializing in sculpture, and later went to graduate school where I completed my major in psychology and a master's degree in teaching art. My good friend Whitney Abt, who was an allbreed judge for the American Cat Fancier's Association and probably knew more about cats than anyone, had been urging me to enter the ACFA judging program. Although I had been interested in the program for a long time, I was just plain scared; I felt I would never know enough to be a good judge, and I was very timid around people. Whitney pushed me into the program, assuring me that I would make a good judge. I was so nervous during my first training session that my hands shook violently and I could not write down the cats' scores. I thought I would never have the courage to judge my first cat show. Somehow I survived my first three shows, and judging has been total pleasure ever since.

In 1979, when the International Cat Association (TICA) was formed, I changed affiliation to become a TICA charter member, as instructor and as director of training and development, and, from 1980 to the present, serving as judging administrator as well. At present I am an allbreed judge, instructor (licensed to train apprentices and to give judging schools and breed seminars) and serve as a genetics instructor and a member of TICA's genetic committee and judiciary committee.

In my work I have had a great deal of difficulty trying to convince people that a frost point bred to another frost point would never bring forth a seal point, no matter what was in the pedigree; that a Siamese out of two Oriental Shorthairs, each carrying the pointed gene, was a Siamese, if the correct type was there; that the earlier Abyssinians were also blue in color and just as much an Abyssinian as a ruddy; that Lynx Point Siamese were Siamese, if the type was there. Or that if the Parti-Color Points were accepted by the Oriental Shorthairs, the Siamese would not be ruined forever because the white spotting gene would get into the gene pool and the Siamese would end up with white feet.

I pressed that the aim of breeders should be for honest pedigrees and that the way to accomplish this was through knowledge. I wanted breeders to understand that if we continue to stay within a limited gene pool, resulting generations are in danger of miniaturization, lack of hybrid vigor, sterility and depression (depression for the cat and the breeder).

People often ask why I stay in cat fancy. I answer that it is like living in a worldwide community, where you have instant acceptance anyplace where there is a cat fancier. I have put most of my life into the world of cat fancy and have never regretted it.

I first met Mr. Tetsu Yamazaki eleven years ago in Seattle, at a cat show. A Japanese man appeared in my judging ring, covered with cameras—that was Tetsu. We talked (with the help of an interpreter) and had dinner together that night. I liked Tetsu instantly and invited him to visit me in New Orleans, which he did the following week, staying with me for two weeks. Looking back on that visit, I realize it must have been difficult for Tetsu, as I spoke no Japanese and he spoke no English. But we did not need a spoken language to become fast and good friends. This would be the first of many visits to come.

In 1985, Tetsu announced he was going to do another book on cats and wanted me to write the text. At the time I was living on top of a mountain in southern Oregon, with no electricity. I had only a generator to provide power for my computer, which began to

Norwegian Forest Cat

hum many hours of the day, completely changing the sound of my otherwise silent mountain. The writing took place over a period of three years, and it was necessary for me to make several trips to Japan to look at Tetsu's slides of the cats.

Tetsu's ability to photograph cats is remarkable. He has so much patience with them, and knows instinctively how to handle the cats. He is able to capture and communicate the essence of the cat on film in a fleeting moment. Our hope is for readers to become more familiar with the different breeds of cats, so that if they decide to acquire a pet or a show cat they will have good information on which to base their decision.

One of the goals of a registering body and the breeder is to keep and preserve accurate records. Part of this aim should be to leave a legacy of information about the breeds and colors, and the representatives of the breeds, at a specific point in time. We want to encourage the relationship between cats and humans, because without this interaction the world of cat fancy would not exist!

Tetsu and I offer you this, our book, our legacy of the cat.

Gloria Stephens

The History of the Domesticated Cat

Man and the Cat

The domesticated cat has had an on again, off again relationship with humans throughout history. The cat remains aloof, often misunderstood; it has the potential of returning to a wild state, no longer dependent on man; it may be envied, or, because it does not always give blind love, it may be resented or feared. The cat has been associated with ancient gods, devils and familiars, and attributed with special powers to control human destiny. The obverse of this relationship is the modern cat fancier, who knows, understands and loves the cat, marveling that one has adopted the human for its very own.

Early Ancestry

Forerunners of our domestic cat may have been the European wild cat, *Felis silvestris*, or the African wild cat, *Felis libyca* of ancient Egypt. Another theory is that the Desert Sand Cats were the primary progenitors of *felines domestica* and the famous European "sylvester" was only a secondary contributor. The Desert Sand Cat is a shy little cat with a rough and tumble, rather coarse semi-longhaired coat.

Migration

The earlier forerunner of the domestic cat may have had its origin in the Eocene period, which also produced the ancestor of man. This was miacis, a small, ill-tempered, weasel-like creature resembling today's martens. The descendants of miacis evolved into various families of carnivores; among them are members of the cat family. The civets and genets are cousins of the domestic cat. The original miacis were lynx-sized animals with retractable claws and streamlined bodies. Many species died out during the Ice Age three million years ago; along with homo sapiens some forty species of the cat family survived, among them cheetahs, the felis (smaller cats) and the great cats. All of these except the cheetahs occurred both in the Old and New Worlds. Members of the cat families crossed from one hemisphere to another by the land bridge at the Bering Sea. When this bridge became submerged, the "crossed over" species developed in adaptation to their new environment. Heavier cats, with thicker coats, evolved in the colder regions; the swift, lean cats thrived in warmer climates. Cats did not reach South America until about two million years ago. Antarctica and Australia never had cats.

Cats in Ancient Egypt

The first domestication of the cat was recorded in Egyptian times five thousand years ago. Domestication may have occurred in other places at other times, but we do not have other documentation than the Egyptian paintings, dating to 2000 B.C., showing cats in what appears to be friendly rapport with humans, suggesting some form of domestication. From 2000 B.C., evidence shows that cats were plentiful in Egypt, were well cared for, trained to hunt wild birds and to fish, and were greatly valued for their ability to keep the rodent population under control. So valuable was the cat that laws were made to protect it from harm.

The cat was worshiped in Egypt for more than two thousand years. At first the cat was considered sacred only to the goddess Isis. It later became sacred to the great cat goddess Bastet. Indeed, the earliest portrayals of Bastet showed her as a cat-headed figure. Gradually Bastet became the most important god to all Egyptians, and the cat was held sacred and worshiped with her. The Egyptian word for cat is *mau* which means "to see."

Cats were so greatly loved by the Egyptians that when a cat died, it was mummified by rubbing the body with precious oils and carefully wrapping it in layers of cloth. It was then taken to a special cemetery where the bereaved family would beat gongs and shave off their eyebrows as a sign of mourning. In the twentieth century such a cemetery containing over three hundred thousand mummified cats was discovered at Beni Hassan. In 1907, 190 skulls were presented to the British Museum; most of these skulls represented a particular group of cats, a form of the small African bush cat, which had a tabby body, rings on the tail and the "beetle" or scarab mark between the ears.

Migration from Asia to Europe and Great Britain

From Egypt, the little African bush cat became established in China and India in the semi-wild state. Trade evidently later brought the cat to Italy. The Greeks acquired cats from the Egyptians; the seafaring Phoenicians carried cats on board with them to various parts of their world. It may have been by this means that Britain acquired cats; the Romans, also, brought cats with them to Britain. Cats were needed, as always, to keep rodents in check.

The cat eventually became so valuable in England that in 939 A.D. a kitten was paid for even before it opened its eyes. Once the kitten was old enough to catch mice, the price doubled. Anyone found guilty of killing a cat had to pay its worth in corn, measured by holding the dead animal by the tip of its tail, so that the nose touched the ground. Grain was then poured over it until the whole body was completely covered.

Cats During the Middle Ages

Cats have long been associated with death or with the spirit world. They remained greatly valued until the Middle Ages, when they began to be used in sacrificial rites and were put to death by the thousands. In 1484, Pope Innocent VIII denounced the cat and all who housed it. Many thousands of people, mostly women, were put to death in Germany alone, for merely keeping or protecting cats. Executions also took place in France, and hundreds of thousands of cats were destroyed in ceremonies presided over by priests. (Pagan rituals still persisted, however, and spread to the New World: more than two thousand trials for cat sorcery were held in New England.) The good standing of cats was reinstated as a result of the Black Plague; they were needed to kill the plague-carrying rodents, so once more the cat was allowed to live in relative peace.

Classification of Cats

Cats belong to a well-defined family called the *Felidae*, which includes about thirty-eight recognized species. One method of classification is to determine the structure of the hyoid bone which is at the base of the tongue. In the larger cats this is made primarily of cartilage, allowing the bone to move freely, thus enabling the large cats to roar. When the hyoid bone is fully ossified and rigid, the cats cannot roar; cats with the latter characteristic have been assigned the name or genus *Felis* and are our small cats. The cheetah, which has claws that do not fully retract, has been placed in a genus all its own. To further break down the *Felidae* into genera according to unusual or unique characteristics: clouded leopards, genus *Neofelis*, have very long canine teeth; the lynx, genus *Lynx*, have very short tails and tufted ears; ocelots and Geoffrey's Cat, genus *Leopardus*, have thirty-six instead of thirty-eight chromosomes.

All cats have much in common: they all walk on their toes; the construction of their bodies enables them to move with great speed, although this speed usually cannot be maintained over a long period of time; all cats normally have five toes on the front paws and four on the hind paws, with pads at the base of each toe and a larger pad in the middle; all newborn kittens or cubs are born with fur and are born blind, their eyes sealed shut.

The domestic cats in this book are in the genus *Felis catus*. It should be noted that wild cats of different species cannot interbreed and produce fertile offspring, but feral domestic cats have occasionally interbred with African and European wild cats to produce some offspring that are fertile.

Abyssinian

The cat has survived for thousands of years, through many hardships, but there is sometimes a question as to whether certain breeds can survive the intervention of humans.

Early Cat Shows

The deliberate breeding of cats started just a little over one hundred years ago. The interest in individual breeds has been attributed to an artist and cat lover named Mr. Harrison Weir, who wrote: "I conceived the idea that it would be well to hold Cat Shows, so that different breeds, colours, markings, etc. might be more carefully attended to, and the domestic cat sitting in front of the fire would then possess a beauty and an attractiveness to its owner unobserved and unknown because uncultivated heretofore."

Weir proceeded to lay the early foundations for a cat show, with guidelines for classes, prices, prizes and the "Points of Excellence," a set of standards describing each of the breeds. These early standards were concerned with color and pattern as a means of identifying a breed rather than a type. Only in relatively recent years has the influence of color over type taken second place. In some organizations, a group of cats must have a structural uniqueness different from any other existing breed to be recognized as a breed. Without a structural difference, it is just a variation of an existing breed; spots, color and pattern do not suffice.

The first cat show in Great Britain took place at the Crystal Palace in London, on July 13, 1871; 160 cats were exhibited. Harrison Weir, his brother John Weir and the Reverend J. Macdona were appointed official judges. Other shows followed: in 1873 in Alexandra Palace and in Birmingham; in 1875 a show in Edinburgh had an entry of 560 cats; in that same year the Crystal Palace had "325 pens." Dr. Gordon Stables, an early cat judge, wrote in 1876, "Cat shows are only in their infancy and anyone who chances to have a good cat may nowadays take prizes. In future years there will be no chance work about the matter at all, and only those who study the breeding and rearing of cats in a scientific and sensible manner will be the winners."

In those early shows, most of the cats were shorthairs and were grouped according to color for judging. The first cat show in the United States was held in 1895 at Madison Square Garden in New York City. In 1887, the National Cat Club was formed, with Harrison Weir as its president; this club started keeping a record or studbook of pedigrees. It became the first registering body for the pedigreed cats of the world. The club continued this work until 1910, when the Governing Council of Cat Fanciers (GCCF) was founded and took over the registration of cats. GCCF continues to have a controlling, respected and strong influence.

The cat shows of today have not changed much from the earlier ones. Different countries may have different methods of judging, as some judges do not handle the cats, while others do physically examine them. The standards for the breeds may be slightly or greatly different from country to country, based on aesthetic preferences. The Siamese cat of today, for example, bears little resemblance to the Siamese of twenty years ago. If long is best, then longer is better; if short is best, then shorter is better. If care is not taken, all the breeds could be reduced to modifications of the Siamese and the Persian!

The Impact of the World Wars

Human suffering in both World Wars precluded widespread concern for the survival of purebred cat populations. In order to preserve the existing breeds, English breeders had to outcross to any available breed of cat. This outcrossing brought in unrelated genes specific for a breed. Even now, breeders have been shocked to find, for example, a longhaired kitten in a shorthaired litter where there should have been none. The breeder of Siamese, after many years of breeding nothing but shorthaired Siamese, suddenly gets a longhaired kitten. A sudden mutation? Not likely. It is more probable that a breeder during the war, in desperation to preserve her Siamese bloodlines, used a cat such as a Turkish Angora, thus introducing the longhair gene into the Siamese gene pool. The same could have happened with the Abyssinian, when the longhaired Abyssinian (Somali) makes its appearance.

Possible Extinction of Some Breeds

Various breeds as we know them today have been carefully developed. It is hoped, however, that this manipulation and control does not ultimately lead a breed to extinction. A forewarning of this might be the progressively smaller number of certain breeds exhibited in shows, smaller litters, and fewer cats being registered. Certain breeds will ultimately face extinction if intelligent and knowledgeable intervention does not take place. Gene pools are too small. Some organizations put unrealistic, limiting restrictions on acceptable outcrosses for specific breeds, forcing breeders to constantly double up on genes, risking each time the pairing of undesirable, unhealthy and even lethal genes. All of this is done in the name of preserving the "purebred cat," not wanting to contaminate the "pure" gene pool. But as long as there are recessive genes, as long as man manipulates, as long as cats breed freely in nature, there is no such thing as a purebred cat.

The one thing that must never change is our love, acceptance and respect for the cat; the human ego must never put the winning of awards above the welfare of the cat!

The Basics of Genetics

Principles of Coloration or What Makes a Black Cat Blue?

Phaeomelanin and Eumelanin Pigments, Tabby Genes

There are two basic principles of domestic feline genetics:

1. A domestic cat is red or it is not red, based on phaeomelanin (red-yellow) or eumelanin (black-brown) pigment granules in the hair shaft.
2. All domestic cats have tabby genes in their genotype.

Cells

The cell is common to every living thing. Within the cell is a command center called the nucleus and within the nucleus are chromosomes. On these chromosomes are genes like beads on a string. Genes contain the blueprint for an individual. Every living thing on earth has the same atoms. How these identical atoms are arranged is what makes a cat different from a dog, or a man different from a flower.

There are two types of cells: body and sex cells. Body cells must replicate to produce cells exactly like the parent cells, to produce skin, hair, heart, muscle, and so forth. Each cell in the domestic cat has thirty-eight chromosomes, or nineteen pairs. The sex cells (the egg in the female and sperm in the male) have nineteen pairs each. When the sperm fertilizes the egg, the full complement of thirty-eight chromosomes is restored.

Genes or Alleles

Genes are instructors of development for a particular trait and are considered to be units of heredity. A gene is a group of nucleotide bases held together on the DNA molecule. There are two copies of each gene, one for each paired chromosome (S/S; S/s; or s/s).

Gene Interaction

Genes interact together, thus altering expressivity. Genes may be modified by environment. There may be incomplete dominance (the recessive is able to exert influence over the dominant: S/s) within a mutated (allelic) system. Genes

Siamese

may be modified by interaction of multiple minor genes called polygenes or modifiers. Color development is greatly influenced by polygenes, giving variations in color and patterns.

Masking Genes

Some genes mask (cover) other genes: phaeomelanin masks eumelanin; dominant white masks eumelanin and/or phaeomelanin; nonagouti masks tabby.

Chromosomes

The chromosomes within the nucleus of a cell are large DNA molecules consisting of paired nucleotide bases which make up the genes. These bases spell out codes for the messenger RNA, which in turn takes the codes to a place in the cell where protein synthesis takes place.

Each species has a specific number of chromosomes. Chromosomes come in pairs; each gene or allele has a specific address on the chromosome. Each individual has identical chromosomes in each body cell; these chromosomes are unique to that individual and may serve as a genetic fingerprint.

Dominant and Recessive Genes

Genes are dominant or recessive. In the homozygous state (B/B or b/b) the same message is sent and received. In the heterozygous state (B/b) the dominant gene (B) is in control; the recessive (b) is carried and may have little or no effect over (B). A recessive gene may be "carried" undetected for many generations. Undesirable recessive genes are very difficult to eliminate because of their recessivity.

Sex-Linked Red

Phaeomelanin is sex-linked; it is positioned on the "X" chromosome. Its mate, the smaller "y" chromosome, does not have a color; it determines the sex of the cat.

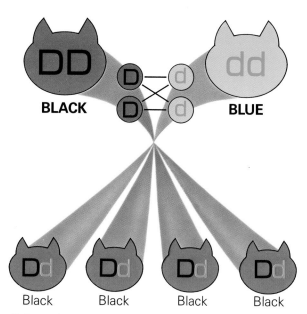

To Test a Genotype: The dominant gene D controls dense pigmentation, and its recessive gene d/d controls maltesing or dilution. This is accomplished by clustering the dense pigmentation granules when they are deposited in the hair shaft. If two cats, heterozygous (D/d), are bred together, the kittens from this breeding are as follows: 1 (D/D)=dense pigmentation; 2 (D/d)=dense pigmentation carrying the recessive maltesing gene; 1 (d/d)=maltesed.

Pigment or Melanin Synthesis

Pigment granule synthesis is under the influence of the heat-sensitive enzyme tyrosinase. The darker the color, the more insensitive to heat: black is more insensitive to heat than chocolate; chocolate is more insensitive to heat than cinnamon. Darker bands of pigments may be lighter near the base of the hair and almost white at the roots, due to the warmth of the skin.

"Pointed" kittens are born white; color is not yet developed because the kittens were kept warm in the mother's uterus. Color will begin to develop on the coldest parts of the body—the extremities (points). The warmer body area will develop little color.

Pigment-producing cells are formed when the kitten is an embryo, and migrate to assigned body areas. White spotting is neither predictable nor controllable. Birmans may have a modifier to help keep a white pattern restricted to the feet.

Melanin Production

The color(s) in hair, skin and eyes are caused by the presence of melanin, which is formed after enzyme biochemical reactions of tyrosinase. Tyrosinase synthesis takes place in the melanocyte, and is the biochemical basis of melanin formation. Melanin is deposited in the form of granules which vary in shape, size and arrangement, giving a variety of colors. There are two kinds of melanin in synthesis: eumelanin and phaeomelanin.

Eumelanin (black-based melanin) granules are thought to be spherical in shape and absorb al-

Abyssinian/Somali

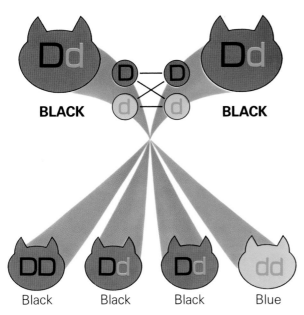

BLACK | **BLACK**

DD — Black
Dd — Black
Dd — Black
dd — Blue

The maltesing gene must have color to work on; it cannot work on itself. Therefore, if we add color (it could be black, chocolate, cinnamon or red), we would have the following results: 1 (B/B, D/D) = black; 2 (B/B, D/d) = black, carrying blue; 1 (B/B, d/d) = blue.

most all light. Phaeomelanin (red-based melanin) granules are thought to be elongated "footballs" in shape, and refract light in the red-orange-yellow range.

Melanin is evenly deposited in the hair shaft where there is continuous enzyme production, starting at the tip of the hair and continuing to the last production, the lower portion of the hair, which sometimes is pale in color.

Dense Pigmentation

Dense pigmentation (D/D) determines the density of color. Pigment granules are deposited separately and individually in the hair shaft. Light is reflected from the entire surface, giving a darker color.

Maltesing

In maltesing, also referred to as dilution (d/d), granules are deposited in clusters in the hair shaft, allowing less light reflection, resulting in a lighter color. Any of the densely pigmented phaeomelanistic or eumelanistic colors may be maltesed.

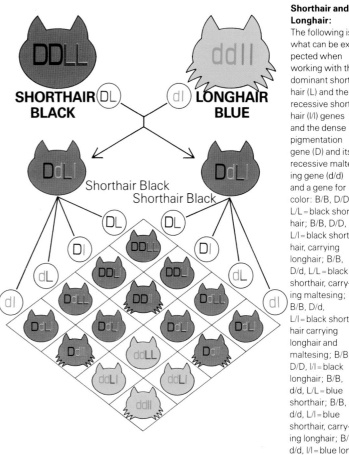

SHORTHAIR BLACK (DDLL) × **LONGHAIR BLUE** (ddll)

Shorthair Black (DdLl) — Shorthair Black (DdLl)

Shorthair and Longhair: The following is what can be expected when working with the dominant shorthair (L) and the recessive shorthair (l/l) genes and the dense pigmentation gene (D) and its recessive maltesing gene (d/d) and a gene for color: B/B, D/D, L/L = black shorthair; B/B, D/D, L/l = black shorthair, carrying longhair; B/B, D/d, L/L = black shorthair, carrying maltesing; B/B, D/d, L/l = black shorthair carrying longhair and maltesing; B/B, D/D, l/l = black longhair; B/B, d/d, L/L = blue shorthair; B/B, d/d, L/l = blue shorthair, carrying longhair; B/B, d/d, l/l = blue longhair (black maltesed).

American Curl

Agouti Allele

The agouti (A) is responsible for banded or ticked hair. The agouti allele is an on-off system of pigment synthesis, a speeding up and slowing down of production. "On" will produce the darker agouti band; "off" will produce shredded yellow to orange granules. The agouti banded hairs surround the tabby pattern, making it visible to the eye.

Non-Agouti Allele

The solid colors or "self" colors are the result of the non-agouti gene (a/a). This gene inactivates the formation of the yellow agouti band. It is an "on" production of eumelanin and can only work in conjunction with eumelanin. Solid red-cream hair is not genetically possible. In red or cream cats the yellow agouti band is not affected by the non-agouti gene. The non-agouti gene is not operative on phaeomelanin. In red or cream cats, red and yellow bands (agouti banding) are present, allowing the tabby pattern to be seen. All red and creams will display tabby pattern to a lesser or greater degree. For a "solid red" to appear solid, the cat should be an agouti tabby and highly rufoused. Solid color is a result, for example, of a black band followed by another black band and so on. The eye sees the color as being one solid color, not as a series of bands.

Phaeomelanin

Red and cream are the product of phaeomelanin synthesis which is chemically different from eumelanin: the granules are a different shape than those of eumelanin. The exact biochemical synthesis of melanin in the domestic cat has not been completely examined. It would appear that red converts all eumelanin to phaeomelanin, or, when phaeomelanin synthesis is taking place, eumelanin is not synthesized; areas that would have been eumelanin are phaeomelanin. The yellow agouti band may be shredded phaeome-

Pigmentation and Maltesing

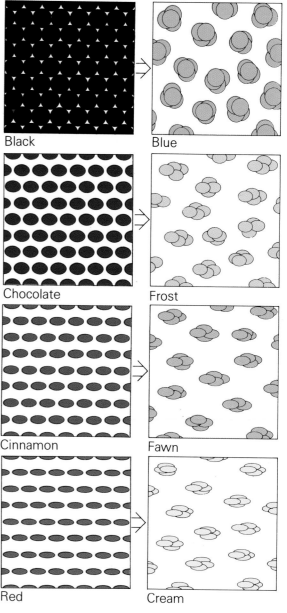

Black Blue

Chocolate Frost

Cinnamon Fawn

Red Cream

lanin, not affected by the non-agouti gene. Red, in dense pigmentation, results in a deep, rich, clear orange-red. Cream is maltesed red, a buff cream color.

Russian Blue

ON
The formation of pigment is rapid; color becomes black.

OFF
Pigment forms slowly; color is in the yellow-to-orange range.

ON
Formation of pigment becomes rapid; color becomes black.

OFF
Formation of pigment slows; color is in the yellow-to-orange range.

Agouti

*Oriental Shorthair
Fawn/Chocolate*

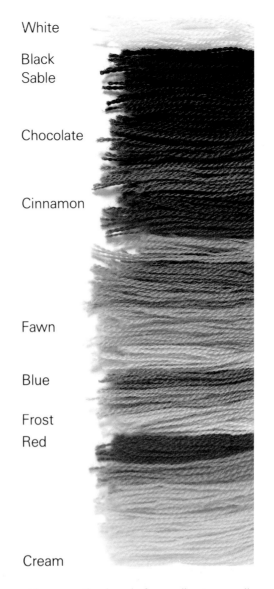

White

Black
Sable

Chocolate

Cinnamon

Fawn

Blue

Frost
Red

Cream

Eumelanin

Black or ebony is the result of eumelanin synthesis. Silvering may be responsible for "blue" jet black color. Blue is maltesed black. Most color standards call for a pale blue color, the paler the better. Chocolate or chestnut is a medium to dark brown color of dense pigmentation, and is a dilution, recessive to black; it is also referred to as chocolate dilution. There may be a reduction or a smaller number of granules deposited in the hair shaft. Cinnamon, or light chocolate, is of dense pigmentation and is a terra-cotta or burnt sienna color. Cinnamon is an allele at the (B) locus; cinnamon is recessive to chocolate and black. Frost is maltesed chocolate and is also called lilac or lavender; it is a frost-gray, dove or light taupe gray. Fawn is coffee and cream or caramel color; a warm pinkish buff. It may be a maltesing of cinnamon or the result of a dominant modifier and a maltesing gene.

Tabby

The tabby pattern consists of two components: the agouti gene and the genes for tabby pattern. Other conditions will allow the pattern to be seen: the red gene; some young kittens who will become solid colored; "smoking" or when smoking and shaded genes are in heterozygous form to produce a smoke tabby (Egyptian Mau, for example).

The ground color of the "wild" tabby is rather unremarkable; it has not been rufoused (an enhancement of ground color caused by the rufousing polygene). Many show cats, the reds and the brown tabbies, are rufoused or golden, resulting in a rich warm apricot ground color.

The agouti (Abyssinian tabby or ticked tabby) appears to be dominant to other patterns and is the least expression of the tabby pattern with the markings on the head: frown lines, pencil markings and the "M" on the forehead. The body should be clear of markings, with no bars or rings. This pattern is excellent to work with if a

Persian Red

non-tabbied body is desired such as the reds and creams, tortoiseshells and lynx points.

The mackerel tabby pattern is in the form of lines. The classic tabby pattern is a combination of lines and circles or bull's eyes. The spotted tabby pattern is believed to be caused by the action of a modifier on the mackerel or classic tabby pattern, causing the lines to be broken up to form spots, as the spotted tabby pattern may follow either the mackerel or the classic tabby pattern. All tabbies will have the characteristic "M" on their foreheads.

Torbie

A torbie, also called a patched tabby or a tortie tabby, is a tortoiseshell that has been tabbied by adding the agouti gene (the tabby pattern already being in its genotype). If the cat is a torbie, the eumelanistic areas must be tabbied. If the cat is a tortie, the eumelanistic areas are a solid color. Due to the non-agouti gene not being operative on phaeomelanin, the phaeomelanin areas of the tortie may appear tabby. Most torties or torbies are females. If, on rare occasion, a male tortie or torbie is seen (XXy), he is usually sterile. Eumelanin and phaeomelanin will form the continuous genotype tabby pattern in the torbie.

White

White Spotting

The white spotting gene (S) is responsible for white with color patterns. It is a dominant gene, and has incomplete dominance in the heterozy-

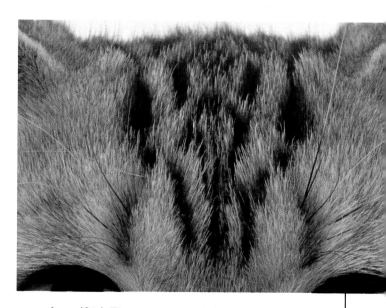

gous form (S/s). There are several theories about the white spotting gene. It may prevent migration and colonization of melanaphores, thus preventing melanin from reaching certain cells or groups of cells. Or, cells (melanoblasts) migrate from the neural crest but fail to survive, thus preventing melanin production in certain cells or groups of cells. (This may be responsible for deafness in the blue eye side of the head; eye color may be blue or odd-eye.) White spotting ranges from a low grade mitted pattern to a medium grade bi-color pattern to the high grade harlequin or Van pattern.

Dominant White

White is not a color, but the absence of color, the masking of all colors and patterns. Color and pattern genes may be present in the genotype but

Mackerel Tabby
(Scottish Fold)

Spotted Tabby
(Egyptian Mau)

Abyssinian Tabby
(Abyssinian)

Classic Tabby
(American Shorthair)

may not be expressed if dominant white is present. Breeding a white cat to a white cat is like opening Pandora's box, as there might be a full spectrum of color and patterns in the kittens. Dominant white kittens may have a spot of color on the top of the head. This is the masked color "breaking through"; the color spot usually disappears after twelve to eighteen months.

It has been theorized that due to the domination of (W), pigment cells are not allowed to migrate, therefore, no pigment is formed, resulting in "white" hairs. Another theory is that certain genes stop the production of hair color as soon as it is started; the growing hairs, in this case, would be empty hair shafts containing no color granules.

The dominant white gene has been used to produce "foreign" whites or white Oriental Shorthairs with blue eyes. The Orientals with the richest blue eyes may be masked chocolate points!

Deafness is usually not associated with the dominant white gene, but with the white spotting gene. A white cat may be a dominant white and white spotted; white spots on white are not

Persian White

visible. Eye color can be copper, gold, orange, blue, green or odd-eye. Copper-eyed whites appear to have been bred copper-eyed to copper-eyed for so many generations that the chances of other eye colors appearing have diminished.

Shaded

Tipping

Theories on tipping include that it may be an effect of the width of the yellow band, influencing the amount of melanin deposited in the tips of hair; that it is the result of the action of the inhibitor gene, an allele not at the albino locus; that smoke and silver are the same allele and are the

Genetic Symbols

Wild Type		Mutants	
Symbol	Name	Symbol	Name
A	Agouti	a/a	Non-Agouti
B	Black	b/b	Chocolate
		b^l/b^l	Cinnamon, light chocolate
C	Full color	c^b/c^b	Sepia
		c^s/c^s	Pointed
		c^a/c^a	White coat, not to be confused with dominant white or white spotting
		c^a/c^a	Albino
		c^b/c^s	Mink
D	Dense pigmentation	d/d	Maltesed pigmentation, dilution
fd/fd	Normal ears	Fd	Folded ears
		Ac	Curled ears
Hr	Normal coat	hr/hr	Almost hairless
L	Short hair	l/l	Longhair
M	Manx, taillessness	m/m	Normal tail
o/o	Normal pigment, not orange	O	Sex-linked orange
pd/pd	Normal number of toes	Pd	Polydactyl (extra toes)
R	Normal coat (length & type)	r/r	Cornish Rex
		re/re	Devon Rex
s/s	Normal color, no white	S	Piebald white spotting
T	Mackerel tabby pattern	T^a	Agouti tabby pattern
		t^b/t^b	Classic tabby pattern
w/w	Normal color, full color	W	Dominant white, masking gene
wh/wh	Normal coat (texture)	Wh	Wirehair

Mitted (Ragdoll)

Bi-Color (British Shorthair)

Van (Turkish Van)

result of the action of one gene, the inhibitor gene. Other theories suggest that tipping alleles are at the albino locus—if so, tipped sepia, pointed, or mink may not be possible; chinchilla or shaded cats are the result of a modifier working on the tabby pattern; smoke is a separate gene and is capable of whitening the undercolor without the presence of the tipping or silvering gene; smoke only works in the presence of non-agouti, therefore only solids and torties may be smoked—a smoke tabby is not possible; tipping genes only control the amount of melanin deposited, therefore a smoke tabby is possible.

Chinchilla/Shaded/Smoke

The undercolor or undercoat may be silvered (chinchilla/shaded silver) or may not be silvered (chinchilla/shaded golden). A chinchilla cat, if silvered, will appear to be almost white, a sparkling white with only one eighth to one quarter of the tips of the hairs showing any color. A shaded cat will appear to have a mantle of color thrown over its back with one third to one half of the tips of the hairs showing color. The smoke cat appears to be of a solid color until the cat moves and the hair is parted to reveal the white undercolor with three quarters of the tips of the hairs showing color. A chinchilla or shaded cat will have green eyes; a smoke cat will have orange, copper or gold eyes; "pewters" will be shaded black with orange eyes.

Full Color

(C/-) is responsible for full color expression, allowing full color to develop throughout the body; the head, body, legs, feet and tail all have approximately the same distribution of color whether the cat is a solid, tabby, tortie, or shaded. Eye color will be gold to copper or green.

The enzyme tyrosinase A is not destroyed quite as fast as it is produced, thus allowing full color development. The allele mutates into subsequent color restrictive pointed alleles.

Persian Shaded Silver

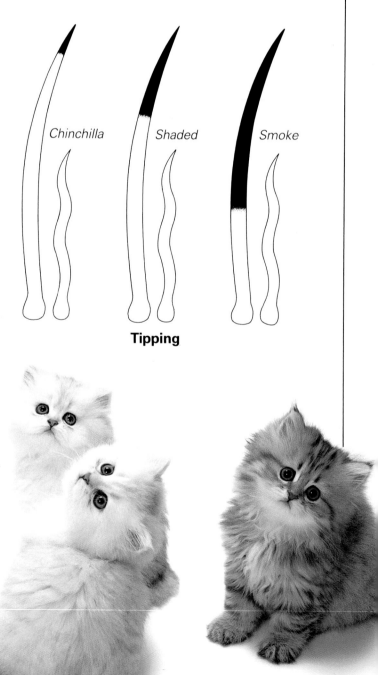

Chinchilla *Shaded* *Smoke*

Tipping

Persian Shaded Silver/Shaded Golden

Pointed

Sepia Color

With c^b/c^b sepia melanin production:

Black	→	seal sepia or sable
Chocolate	→	sepia chocolate/champagne
Blue	→	blue sepia, blue
Cinnamon	→	cinnamon sepia
Fawn	→	fawn sepia
Frost	→	frost sepia/platinum
Red	→	red sepia
Cream	→	cream sepia

Points are present but are not easily seen on darker colors; points are easily seen on dilutes and maltesed colors.

Eye color is copper to gold or yellow; the pigment in front of the eye is reduced, changing copper to gold or yellow; the browning effect of eye pigment is not in operation. The enzyme tyrosinase A^1 is more temperature sensitive.

Pointed Color

With c^s/c^s, color is restricted to the points; body color is a very pale version of points:

Black	→	seal point
Chocolate	→	chocolate point
Blue	→	blue point
Cinnamon	→	cinnamon point
Fawn	→	fawn point
Frost	→	frost point
Red	→	red point
Cream	→	cream point

Eye color is blue; no pigment is deposited in the front of the iris, so only blue light is reflected. The true eye color is masked; the pigment could be copper, green, or gold. Tyrosinase A^{11} is even more heat sensitive.

Mink Color

With c^b/c^s, mink colors are produced by combining sepia and pointed colors, for dark points, body color slightly lighter than the points, and greenish-blue eyes:

Himalayan Seal Point

Black	→	seal mink or natural mink
Chocolate	→	chocolate mink or champagne mink
Blue	→	blue mink
Cinnamon	→	cinnamon mink or honey mink
Fawn	→	fawn mink
Frost	→	frost mink or platinum mink
Red	→	red mink
Cream	→	cream mink

It is believed that any of the pointed cats may be tabbied, tortied, silvered or tipped.

Burmese Sable

Tonkinese Natural Mink

Siamese Chocolate Point

Persian Tortoiseshell

Blue-Eyed White and Albino

With c^a/c^a, results are white with blue eyes, not the same as blue-eyed dominant white; there is an almost complete "burning" out of tyrosinase. With c/c, the result is albino. A true albino has pink eyes. Albinism (colorlessness) is caused by the lack of pigment production; the essential enzyme tyrosinase is not produced or is destroyed as it is produced.

Tortoiseshell

The tortoiseshell pattern is a mosaic of eumelanin and phaeomelanin in patches of color, fitted together like a picture puzzle. The brindled pattern is preferred in the British Shorthair.

In the embryonic state, any female cell has two "X" chromosomes; only one may be active. One "X" chromosome (carrying either the phaeomelanin or eumelanin color) is inactivated in the cell early in development. The color on the inactivated chromosome will never develop. The active color on the "X" chromosome will be synthesized, and as these cells multiply, patches of phaeomelanin or eumelanin will develop, forming the tortoiseshell pattern.

Tortie Colors

Tortoiseshell colors consist of black and red patches, or, in chocolate and cinnamon torties, patches of chocolate or cinnamon and red. Some organizations accept black, red and cream. Cream is not correct as cream is maltesed red; this lighter area is actually the agouti ticking, giving the appearance of cream. If the tortoiseshell is an agouti tabby, the only tabby pattern will be on the extremities.

Maltesed Torties

Any of the dense pigmented tortie or torbie patterns may be maltesed. Colors are blue, frost, or fawn torties, having patches of blue, frost, or fawn and cream.

Breeding Chart for Phaeomelanin and Eumelanin

The gene for red pigment is on the "X" chromosome and is sex-linked. The following chart may be used for determining the exact sex and color in tortie breeding; the chart may also be used for tabby, sepia, mink pointed, tipped, white spotted

Red × Red			Black × Black	
	X^R	X^R		X^B	X^B
X^R	X^R X^R Red ♀	X^R X^R Red ♀	X^B	X^B X^B Black ♀	X^B X^B Black ♀
Y	X^R Y Red ♂	X^R Y Red ♂	Y	X^B Y Black ♂	X^B Y Black ♂

Black female × Red male			Red female × Black male	
	X^B	X^B		X^R	X^R
X^R	X^B X^R Tortie	X^B X^R Tortie	X^B	X^R X^B Tortie	X^R X^B Tortie
Y	X^B Y Black ♂	X^B Y Black ♂	Y	X^R Y Red ♂	X^R Y Red ♂

Tortie × Red male			Tortie × Black male	
	X^B	X^R		X^B	X^R
X^R	X^B X^R Tortie	X^R X^R Red ♀	X^B	X^B X^B Black ♀	X^R X^B Tortie
Y	X^B Y Black ♂	X^R Y Red ♂	Y	X^B Y Black ♂	X^R Y Red ♂

CODE

XX = Female   B = Black
XY = Male   R = Red
BR = Tortoiseshell

Persian Tortoiseshell and White

or maltesed cats. Consideration must be given for the heterozygous in predicting the genotype of the offspring: tabby x tabby may produce solids; black x black may produce pointed.

Mutations

Mutations occur when part of the DNA molecule is altered or changed due to "copying" errors or environmental influences. There may be several mutations of the same gene, which will form an allelic system that may cause a different hair texture, a variation on the color or pattern, and more. Some are beautiful, some are helpful, and some are lethal.

Hairlessness (hr/hr), represented by the Sphynx breed, is recessive to full coat; incomplete dominance may result in variations of hairlessness.

Folded ears (Fd/-), represented by Scottish Folds, appear to be dominant to normal ears, and appear to be crippling when homozygous.

Devon (re/re) and Cornish Rex (r/r) are two separate "rexing" genes; each one is recessive to a straight coat.

The taillessness of the Manx is caused by a dominant gene (M) and is lethal in the homozygous dominant form, which causes the kittens to die before birth due to incomplete development of the spine. It appears to be safe in the heterozygous form.

The curled ear (Ac/-) of the American Curl appears to be a dominant gene. So far there has not been enough data to prove or disprove that curl-

Manx

Sphynx

Cornish Rex

ing of the ear is connected with folding of the ear. Both are affected by a stiffening of the cartilage in the ears.

Other Colors and Patterns

Silver appears to eliminate yellow or shredded material, thus eliminating the yellow ground color, undercolor, or undercoat.

Silver tabby: the silver gene may cause color to intensify. The yellow-orange bands and ground color are silvered. It is possible to silver any of the tabby or torbie patterns. Eye color in the United States is green; gold- or orange-eyed silver tabbies may be recognized in other countries.

Golden is an undetermined polygene or allele, a color enhancer of non-silvered ground color, non-silvered undercolor, and a non-silvered undercoat. It would appear that the granules in the yellow-orange band have been altered to an apricot color. The rufous and golden gene may be the same gene or the result of a group of polygenes and may be thermolabile. Most goldens have green eyes. Tipped cats, tabbies, torties and smokes may be made golden.

Tortie and white, or calico: calico is a name also given to the tortie and white pattern and refers to a white cat with small patches of color as if dropped or painted on by a paintbrush. Particolor is another name given to a tortie and white cat with two thirds color and one third white.

Torbie and white, or caliby: caliby is another name given to a torbie and white.

Scottish Fold

Body Type

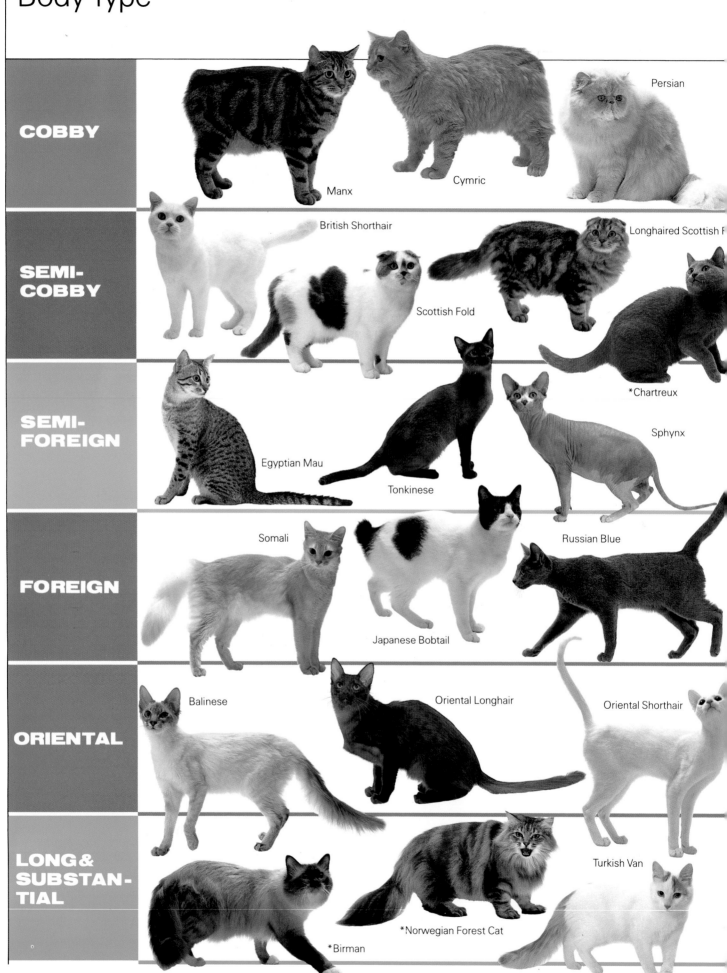

COBBY

Manx

Cymric

Persian

SEMI-COBBY

British Shorthair

Scottish Fold

Longhaired Scottish F

*Chartreux

SEMI-FOREIGN

Egyptian Mau

Tonkinese

Sphynx

FOREIGN

Somali

Japanese Bobtail

Russian Blue

ORIENTAL

Balinese

Oriental Longhair

Oriental Shorthair

LONG & SUBSTANTIAL

*Birman

*Norwegian Forest Cat

Turkish Van

Cats of different breeds are classified by certain physical types according to attributes such as length of body and bone structure. In principal, cats are classified as either oriental or cobby, but in this book they have been described in further detail.

Exotic Shorthair

Himalayan

Burmese

Burmese

American Shorthair

Korat

American Wirehair

Havana

Devon Rex

American Curl

Singapura

Turkish Angora

Abyssinian

Siamese

Cornish Rex

Ocicat

Ragdoll

Maine Coon

*Chartreux: Semi-cobby body, slender legs   *Birman/Norwegian Forest Cat: Medium-long body

Color and Pattern

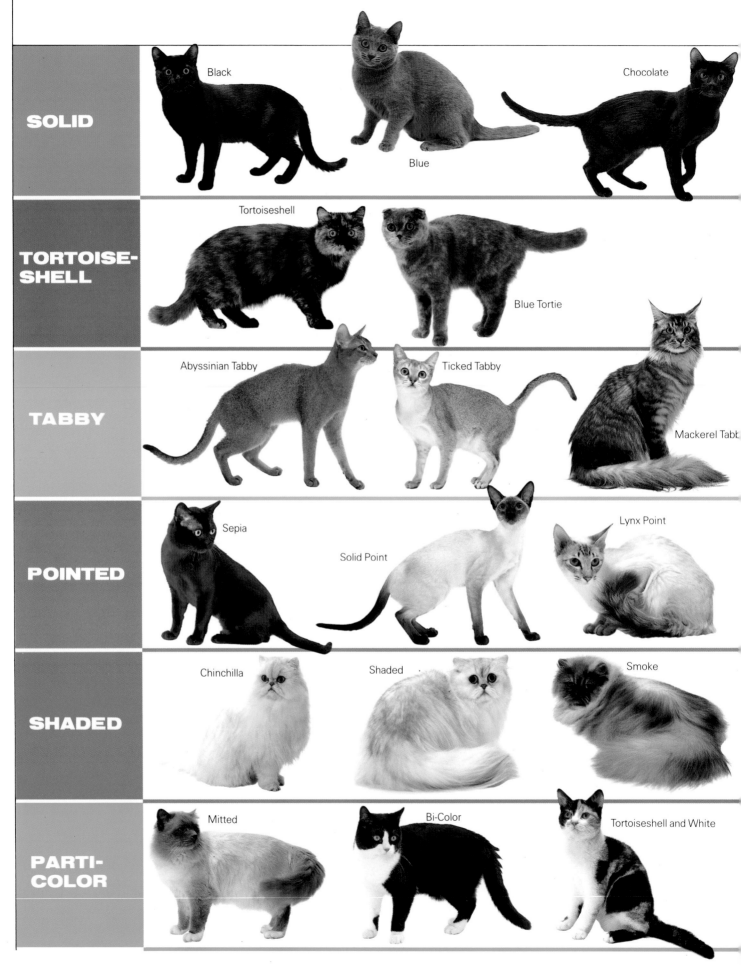

SOLID

Black

Blue

Chocolate

TORTOISE-SHELL

Tortoiseshell

Blue Tortie

TABBY

Abyssinian Tabby

Ticked Tabby

Mackerel Tabb

POINTED

Sepia

Solid Point

Lynx Point

SHADED

Chinchilla

Shaded

Smoke

PARTI-COLOR

Mitted

Bi-Color

Tortoiseshell and White

The cat is basically tabby. The presence of various genes causes the change to solid, tortoiseshell, pointed or shaded coloration. If the dominant white gene is present, color and pattern are masked; the young cat will develop from parti-colored to pure white.

Frost

Red

Cream

White

Spotted Tabby

Classic Tabby

Torbie

Tortie Point

Mink

Tabby & White

Van

Eye Color

The genetics of eye color are not clearly understood. Eye color is not a substance but an effect produced by reflection of light on different materials. Melanin accounts for the color differences by determining the concentration, granule shape and deposit. Eye color is determined by the melanin or lack of melanin in the front or back of the iris.

Blue eyes result from an absence of pigment in front of the iris and brownish melanin scattered in the back of the iris; the optical effect of blue occurs through reflection and dispersion of light rays.

Green eyes result from a dilute brown or yellow pigment in front of the iris and brownish melanin scattered in back; yellow pigment is superimposed on a "blue" background, producing a green effect. The shade of green depends on the amount and kind of melanin laid down in front.

Hazel eyes result from the addition of a little more pigment in front and rear of the iris, creating a grayish yellow, or yellow-flecked-with-green effect.

Copper, gold or orange eyes occur when the front of the iris is filled with pigment; no reflection can be seen as the iris is partially or completely opaque.

White spotting and pointed genes produce a blue effect; the mink gene prevents full pigmentation and scatters granules, producing a blue-green effect; the sepia gene prevents full pigmentation, resulting in a gold effect.

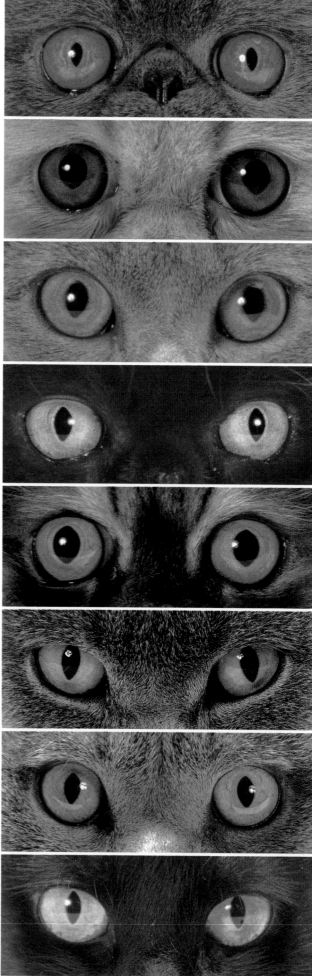

COPPER

ORANGE

GOLD

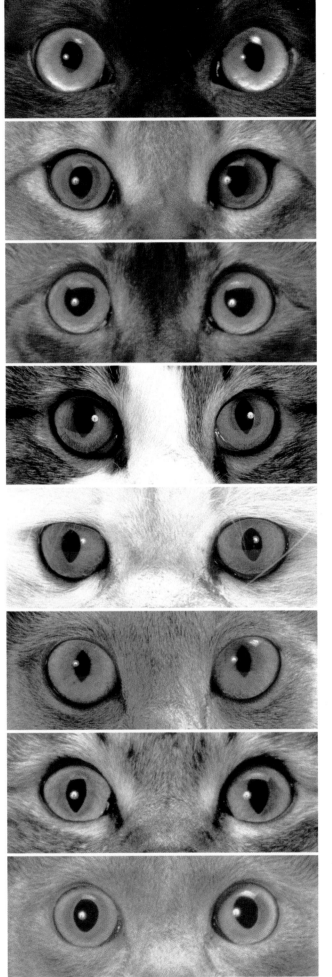

HAZEL

GREEN

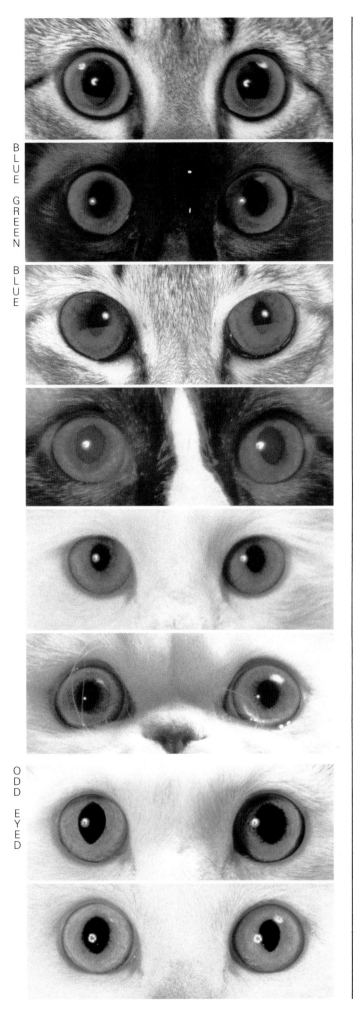

BLUE
GREEN

BLUE

ODD
EYED

Abyssinian
Somali
American Curl
American Shorthair
American Wirehair
Birman
British Shorthair
Burmese
Bombay
Chartreux
Cornish Rex
Devon Rex

PROFILE OF THE CAT: 37 BREEDS

Egyptian Mau
Havana
Japanese Bobtail
Korat
Maine Coon
Manx
Cymric
Norwegian Forest Cat
Ocicat
Persian
Exotic Shorthair
Himalayan
Ragdoll
Russian Blue
Scottish Fold
Longhaired Scottish Fold
Siamese
Balinese
Oriental Shorthair
Oriental Longhair
Singapura
Sphynx
Tonkinese
Turkish Angora
Turkish Van

The age and sex are indicated for each
cat pictured. For example, ♂ 3·10 would mean
the cat is a 3-year, 10-month-old male.

Abyssinian/Somali

The Abyssinian cat is a bit like a miniature cougar and the Somali is rather like a red fox. The ruddy version has a radiant, dazzling color; the sorrel, a flaming burnt-orange color; the blue, a mixture of soft blue and apricot sherbet; the fawn, a mixture of pinkish beige and oatmeal. These elegant, regal animals are among the aristocrats in the world of cat fancy, lithe and panther-like in activity, stately in appearance and endowed with the grace of a dancer. The large, almond-shaped eyes mesmerize all who look into them.

Origin

The Abyssinian may be one of the oldest breeds of domesticated cats, but like so many of our recognized breeds, its exact origin is unknown. Some believe the Abyssinian is a direct descendant of the sacred cat of Egypt, based on characteristic outlines seen on ancient Egyptian paintings and sculptures. These pictures look very much like the Abyssinian and Egyptian Mau of today. According to one story, soldiers returning to England in the 1800s from Ethiopia (Abyssinia) brought cats with them from that country, hence the name Abyssinian.

The contemporary Abyssinian has been carefully developed for color, pattern and type. It has a long body, large ears and eyes and a smooth, resilient coat.

Agouti Pattern

The Abyssinian and Somali are accepted only in the agouti tabby pattern. The gene, which is dominant to the other tabby patterns, is the least expression of the tabby gene, not permitting a tabby pattern to be developed on the body. The tabby pattern is expressed on the head in the form of pen-

Abyssinian Head: modified wedge; rounded contours. Ears: large. Eyes: large; almond. Coat: shorthair. Pattern: agouti tabby. Colors: ruddy, sorrel, blue or fawn.

Abyssinian Ruddy ♂ 1·02

Abyssinian Ruddy

cil lines, frown marks and an inevitable "M" on the forehead. This gene is, however, also responsible for the ticked tabby pattern wherein leg bracelets, necklaces and tail rings are desirable, though all of these are strictly forbidden on the Abyssinian or Somali. Strict breeding practices had to be followed to eliminate these traits. White lockets in the neck and groin area were seen years ago but are seldom found on the show Abyssinian of today. All of these "bad" markings such as white lockets may bring a disqualification or a withholding of awards in a show. Mouse coat, where the hairs are a dark color next to the skin, is also severely frowned upon; even worse is reversed ticking (the outermost tip of hair is light instead of dark), which will bring an immediate disqualification. The Abyssinian, due to its ticked fur, has also been called the "bunny" or "rabbit" cat.

Abyssinian Sorrel ♂ 1·04

Abyssinian Blue ♂ 4·01

Color and Pattern

This is not a solid-colored cat, but has instead an ever-changing overlay of intermingled colors. The color bounces around, as there is no one color for the eye to focus on, but a constant change of colors whenever the cat moves. The belly is a beautiful, warm, rich orange or apricot with no agouti banded hairs.

"Thumbprints" are seen on the back of the ears, a carry-over from the wild helping to protect the cat when asleep. These marks look like eyes, making the cat appear to be awake.

Abyssinian Ruddy

Somali Fawn ♂ 2•06

Fawn

The fawn-cinnamon maltesed is the newest color to be recognized. This is a very subtle color, making it difficult for the eye to see the agouti banding. It is a warm pinkish buff, with a powdered effect, ticked with a deeper shade of pinkish buff. The fawn ground color has also been rufoused, producing a delicately warm, soft color. It must be seen to be believed.

Blue

The blue Abyssinian is unique in color, looking like some kind of cat from the future. It is ticked with alternating bands of rich deep blue and apricot; the underside is a solid apricot color. This cat is a relative newcomer to the show ring, though the color has been in the gene pool for a long time. In the United States, early breedings produced blues and ruddies in the same litters. The blues were not considered to be as flashy and were therefore deemed undesirable. Breeders stopped breeding for the color, and championship recognition was not requested for years. The blue Abyssinian now has full championship status in some organizations.

Coat

Unique to the Abyssinian is the required short coat of lustrous sheen consisting of rufoused banding and eumelanistic ticking. The rufousing gene changes drab beige yellow to a brilliant apricot.

Red/Sorrel

The "red" Abyssinian was earlier misnamed due to the effect of the rufous gene. The red Abyssinian does look red. Red, however, is a misleading name, in that it would seem to indicate that the cat is under the influence of the sex-linked red gene. This is definitely not the case. If the red Abyssinian were a sex-linked red, then when a red and a ruddy were bred, some of the resulting kittens would be torbies. When a red and a ruddy are bred, the kittens are either ruddy or cinnamon, not torbies. Closer inspection of the color at the tip of the tail reveals an indication of the tabby pattern color. In the case of the red, it will be found that the color is cinnamon. Also, the so-called red produces a fawn color when maltesed, not cream. Because of this, the Breed Section of the International Cat Association (TICA) voted to rename the color as sorrel.

Somali

The Somali is the "red fox" of cats. It displays the same lively, intelligent interest in its surroundings as does the Abyssinian. Fully coated, brilliantly colored, having lynx ear tipping and a long bushy tail, it is a beautiful cat to behold. The coat is very soft to the touch, very fine in texture; it should be dense and double coated. This cat is extremely slow in developing ticking, as are all longhaired cats, and allowances should be made for kittens and young mature cats.

The Somali is the semi-longhaired version of the Abyssinian. It should have the same body type as the Abyssinian, although some organizations allow Somalis to be of semi-foreign type, stating that the body conformation should be between the extremes of the cobby and svelte lengthy types.

General Description and Judging

The Abyssinian and Somali are considered to be among the most difficult breeds to judge, as there are no exaggerated features. The head is a modified wedge with gentle, rounded contours. The ears are strikingly large. The large, expressive, almond-shaped eyes are slanted toward the lower base of the ear. The foreign-typed body is well-developed yet slim in appearance. The cat stands tall on slender legs, of which the hind legs are higher than those in front; the back is slightly arched, giving the appearance of a cat about to spring. The coat is resilient and of fine texture and sheen.

Temperament

The Abyssinian and Somali should be feral in appearance, yet they are extremely gentle and affectionate by nature. They make excellent companions and are quiet, not overly "talkative," even when in season. These cats are very inquisitive; nothing is too small to escape the adventure of investigation. They show a lively interest in all their surroundings and love to climb, yet very seldom disturb or break things, even when they weave between objects like a skier on a slalom course. Their loose skin helps them get in and out of tight places or human hands with ease. They do not like to be caged, and will pace back and forth, much like a wild animal. These are wonderful cats who seem able to "read" the needs of their favorite person.

Somali Head: modified wedge; rounded contours. Ears: large. Eyes: large; almond. Body: foreign. Coat: semi-longhair. Pattern: agouti tabby. Colors: ruddy, sorrel, blue or fawn.

Somali Sorrel ♀ 2·11

American Curl

The American Curl is different from any other breed, with its innocent look and devilish curled-back ears.

Origin

This breed has been hand built, starting with a mutation in the domestic cat population, a female found in California in 1981. This female's ears were not straight, like other cats' ears, but were curled back. She was found in a neighbor's yard and was adopted by a family who were smitten with her and her curled ears. Named Shulamith, she later presented her new family with kittens which were distributed for careful breeding, with several goals in mind: retention of the curly ears, achieving an individual type, and enlarging their gene pool.

The Longhair American Curl was first exhibited in 1983 and given championship recognition in 1987 by the International Cat Association. Cat breeders had never seen anything like this before, and the American Curl took the world of cat fanciers by storm.

In a litter bearing American Curl kittens, with four to eight kittens in the average litter, fifty percent of these may be Curls. When Curl kittens are four to seven days old, their ears start to become firm and curl backwards on the head. At about six weeks, the kittens enter into a transitional stage and the ear gradually unfurls. At four to six months of age, the curl of the ear sets permanently even though the unfurling process is not completed.

The cartilage in the base of the ears is quite firm, even stiff to the touch. Once seen and felt, this trademark cannot be mistaken for anything else. The curly ears and expressive eyes make this breed a unique cat; a delight to look at and a pleasure to own.

American Curl Black ♀ 1·07

American Curl Black and White ♂ 0·11

*American Curl
Brown Mackerel
Tabby and White* ♂ 0·05

American Curl Head:
modified wedge;
rounded contours.
Ears: medium;
curled back.
Eyes: large;
walnut-shaped.
Body: semi-foreign.
Coat: semi-longhair.

American Curl Shorthair Black ♀ 1·02

General Description and Judging

American Curls are semi-foreign, semi-longhaired cats. The head is a modified wedge with rounded contours. The firm ears are held erect, set on the corners of the head, curving in a gentle curl back from the face, toward the center of the back of the head. The walnut-shaped eyes are large and expressive.

This is a medium-sized cat, and may take two to three years to mature. The body should not be cobby or coarse, nor should it have fine or slender boning or musculature, but should be semi-foreign in type; the legs should be medium-long, the hind legs slightly longer than the forelegs.

The coat is semi-long and flat and should not be bushy. At present only the Longhair American Curl has championship status; the shorthairs are shown in the new breed or color, non-championship class. Longhair American Curls may be registered and shown in any color and in any pattern.

Temperament

American Curls are very healthy, hearty cats. They are intelligent and playful, yet gentle, very much a "people cat," and very affectionate, liking to rub their owner's chin and sit on their owner's shoulders. They even like rough play and seem to truly enjoy the company of young children. They may be quiet, almost pensive in attitude, and not overly active, but remain extremely curious about their surroundings. They require very little grooming since their coat rarely mats. They can be easily trained, even to walk on a leash, or to fetch and retrieve. They retain their whimsical attitude throughout their life, retaining their playful activities well into maturity, giving them a reputation for never growing up.

American Curl Shorthair Seal Lynx Point ♂ 0·09

American Shorthair/American

The American Shorthair is America's "native" shorthair cat. It has willingly adapted to meet the needs of humans, never losing its natural intelligence. It is a strong cat whose temperament suggests great pride and common sense. The American Wirehair is called, by some, the "brillo pad" of cat fancy. Its build is similar to that of the American Shorthair. Its coat has a rather rough, hard feel, and each hair is bent or curled at the end.

Origin

The ancestors of the American Shorthair are thought to be the first domestic felines in the New World, brought from Great Britain by the Pilgrims and other early settlers. The immigrants who followed most certainly brought more cats, as they were needed for rodent control on ships and land; they also served as companions. These cats settled North America right along with the pilgrims and pioneers, and were allowed to breed freely among them-selves. The resulting kittens grew up to be strong, healthy cats who easily adapted to extremes of weather and could survive in the wilderness.

The first registered cat in the genealogy of the American Shorthair actually came from Britain and was born on the first of June, 1900. Later, another cat was sent to the United States from Britain. These two were bred to resident American shorthaired cats; the offspring of these breedings were first called Shorthairs. Later they were called Domestic Shorthairs, and in 1966 were renamed American Shorthairs. In 1904 the first cat of this breed, a male smoke, was registered. In following years breeders worked to set type, colors and patterns. In the late 1930s and 1940s, much progress came with more breeders taking an active interest in perfecting the breed.

In order to keep its natural gene pool, the American Shorthair was allowed for years to breed to cats of unknown pedigree, developing according to whims of nature, aided only very slightly by mankind. Unfortunately, this is no longer true in most organizations. The American Shorthair has only one accepted outcross in TICA: the American Wirehair.

American Shorthair Head: round; square muzzle; slight stop. Ears: medium; wide set. Eyes: medium to large; round. Body: semi-cobby. Coat: shorthair.

American Shorthair Silver Classic Tabby ♀ 0·07

Wirehair

American Shorthair
Silver Classic Tabby ♂ 2·09

General Description and Judging

This cat is a working cat, displaying all the patience of the hunter and the strength of an athlete, in complete control of its environment and its reflexes, being flexible enough to stalk its prey slowly and make the kill quickly. Its powerful legs are long enough to cope with any terrain. The strong muzzle is of adequate length to permit an easy catch, with steel-trap jaws. The all-weather coat is dense, to protect it from rain and cold or skin injuries, but short enough and of hard enough texture to resist matting or becoming tangled in heavy vegetation. No one part of the anatomy is extreme. The general effect is that of a well-trained athlete, with all muscles lean and hard and with great power held in reserve. The females may be less massive than the males.

Medium, strong and hefty are key words. The head is broad and rounded, with full cheeks and a well-developed, medium-short, squarish muzzle which should be well-padded. If the cheeks are not full, and the muzzle not square, the face will be too narrow for the "look" of the American Shorthair. The medium-sized ears are set well apart, as are the medium to large round eyes. In profile, a slight curve runs from the forehead to the medium-short nose. There should not be a break like that of the Persian.

The rectangular body is medium to large in size, with medium boning,

American Shorthair Silver Classic Tabby

American Shorthair Brown Classic Tabby ♂ 0·10

well-muscled and powerful. Legs are of medium or moderate length. The American Shorthair's all-weather short coat is hard, well-bodied, lustrous and close-lying. There should be no sign of a woolly or fluffy undercoat which might suggest Persian in the background.

Silver Tabby

The silver tabby pattern has, for the most part, reached perfection in the American Shorthair. It is a breathtaking contrast of black and sparkling silver. When the hair is parted, a silvery white

American Shorthair
Red Classic Tabby ♂ 0·11

ground color is visible. The classic tabby pattern is a swirl of color, surrounded by very bold, wide bands of the same color. The rings on the tail are usually broad and wide. The silver gene has eliminated all of the yellow ground color, resulting in the sparkling silver-white ground.

It should be noted that an undesirable "tarnishing" (the yellow beige of the ground color of the non-silvered tabby breaking through) may be seen on some silver tabbies, especially in the muzzle area, and especially in the non-pedigreed cats. Breeders have selectively bred to eliminate this tarnishing from their gene pool.

Silver tabby is the accepted name for the black silver tabby. Formerly, only the black silver tabby was recognized for championship status. Now, the silver tabby may be seen in blue, chocolate, frost, fawn, red and cream in some organizations. The silver tabby may also be accepted in any of the tabby patterns.

American Shorthair Cream Classic Tabby ♂ 0·08

Temperament

American Shorthairs make delightful pets. They are intelligent, friendly, affectionate and healthy with an even temperament. They are pleasing to look at, to hold, to touch and communicate with. This is a sweet cat, and, like the Maine Coon and the Norwegian Forest Cat, is gentle and relaxed, mellow and strong. Its hunting instinct is so strong that it will practice or play at hunting in the house.

American Shorthair Shaded Chocolate ♂ 5·09

American Wirehair

Origin

The American Wirehair was a spontaneous mutation that changed the normal straight coat to a coat that is not only springy, dense and resilient, but also coarse and hard to the touch. Guard hairs are bent at the end, forming a hook.

A litter with wirehaired kittens was born in 1967 to a pair of farm cats in up-

American Shorthair Black ♀ 3·06

American Wirehair Tortoiseshell and White ♀ 0•09

state New York. Breeders took over the careful planning of a breeding program by first breeding the male from this litter (who had a wired coat and was named Adam) to his litter mate, whose coat was straight. After two generations, a "true" Wirehair kitten was born in 1969. All American Wirehairs trace their ancestry to Adam. To improve type and vigor, breeders used American Shorthairs in their breeding program.

Judging

The present standard varies little from the American Shorthair standard, with the exception of the coat description. There is, however, a move among some United States breeders to breed for a cat slightly smaller than the American Shorthair.

Temperament

Characteristic of the American Wirehair is activeness, agility and keen interest in its surroundings. Owners describe their cats as muscular and independent. They rule the roost, taking no nonsense from other cats.

American Wirehair Head: round; square muzzle; slight stop. Ears: medium; wide set. Eyes: medium to large; round. Body: semi-cobby. Coat: shorthair, wired hair.

American Wirehair Tortoiseshell and White ♀ 1•00

Birman

The blue-eyed Birman is also known as the sacred cat of Burma. Many legends and mysteries surround the origins of this breed. These majestic, eye-appealing cats are not only sacred as guardians of temples, but sacred and special to their owners.

Origin

The theories of the origin of the Birman include that it came from Southeast Asia, or that it was specifically bred by the French. Or, that the soul of a priest entered the cat, changing the body color to golden and its eyes to a brilliant blue.

Some say that the Birman was introduced to Europe in 1916 from Southeast Asia. In 1925 the Birman was recognized as a breed by the Fédération Féline Française. It is thought that most "sacred cats of Burma" in the world today are descended from the small cat population of the French Birmans. The breed is considered French even though it is not indigenous to France.

The Birman was endangered when only one pair survived during World War II. In order to keep the breed alive, other longhaired and shorthaired breeds were bred to the Birman. The first Birmans to be exported came to the United States in 1959 and to Great Britain in 1965. The Birman was recognized in the United States by the Cat Fancier's Association in 1967 and is now known throughout most of the world.

The Legend of the Sacred Cat

In a temple built on the sides of Mount Lugh, there lived a very old priest. This priest had a long golden beard, which the god Song-Hio was said to have braided. His life was dedicated to the holy service of Tsun-Kyan-Kse, the goddess with the sapphire blue eyes. This goddess supervised the transmigration of souls, allowing some to live again in a holy animal. The priest's favorite cat, Sinh, was always sitting near him. Sinh was a white cat with yellow eyes. The cat's ears, nose, tail and extremities were dark like the color of the earth.

One night a group of bad men came to the temple and murdered the priest. Then the miracle came about: in a bound, Sinh jumped to the throne and sat at the head of his dead master. As the cat sat, the bristly white hair on his spine suddenly became a golden yellow and his golden eyes became blue.

Birman Seal Point ♂ 2·04

The part of his paws touching the dead priest remained white.

Legend has it that when a priest dies, his soul transmigrates into the body of a cat, and upon the cat's death, the transition of the priest's soul into heaven is accomplished.

The story sadly goes on that for the next seven days the loyal cat refused all food and on the seventh day, he died, knowing that only with his death could he take his master into heaven. After this, all the temple cats had a golden mantle and their gold eyes turned blue. And to this day, Birmans have a golden mantle, white feet and blue eyes.

General Description and Judging

The Birman is a semi-longhaired cat with colored points. Among the most distinctive features are the white paws, like white gloves on all four feet. The white on the back foot should come to a point up the back like a gauntlet. The cat is also distinguished by a "Roman"-shaped nose, with the nostrils set low, and a flat forehead. The high cheekbones set off large, almost round, blue eyes.

The Birman is imposing in appearance, medium to large in size, with heavy boning. Birmans are recognized in the parti-color point colors, mitted pattern only. Only the Birmans with perfect or near perfect markings are shown.

Temperament

Birmans are a delight to care for. As their silky fur does not mat, little grooming is required. They are rather outgoing cats. Often they are ready for mating at seven months of age. They give the impression of quiet power and harmony through rather pensive, sweet eyes. Birmans greatly appreciate companionship, especially that of young children, and more readily display happiness than anger. The breed is robust and hardy, reported to be resistant to disease, and easily adaptable to rural or city life.

Birman Frost Point
♀ 0•11

Birman Head: round; Roman nose; definite stop. Ears: medium; wide set. Eyes: large; round; wide set; blue. Body: medium long; substantial. Coat: longhair. Pattern: parti-color point (mitted).

Birman Blue Point ♂ 0•11

British Shorthair

The British Shorthair, Great Britain's working cat, is a very sturdy, muscular cat with a short, plush coat. The breed was developed in Europe from unpedigreed cats.

British Shorthair
Black and White
♂ 1·01

Origin

The British Shorthair's origins are those of the native working cats, the street and yard cats, of Britain. The early British Shorthair and the French Chartreux were of similar type; many breeders think they were originally the same cat. Today, breeders have taken great care to produce two distinct breeds, to be judged separately.

Ancestors of the British Shorthair survived years of superstition and persecution in past centuries, when thousands of cats were killed. It is a marvel that this wonderful, sweet-tempered cat is still around for the whole world to enjoy.

Many shorthairs were shown at the famed Crystal Palace in 1895. They held the limelight for about a year at the shows, until the Persian took over. British Shorthairs were to remain out of favor until the 1930s, when a small number of dedicated breeders took an interest in them. Mr. Harrison Weir, of early cat fancy fame, wrote: "The ordinary garden cat has survived every kind of hardship and persecution. That he exists at all, is tribute to his strength of character and endurance."

In the United States, the early British Shorthairs were called the British Blues, as blue was the only recognized color. They were not as defined as the British Shorthairs of today, and relied more on size and plush coats for their wins than on type. In the 1970s a cat named Mary Poppins caught cat fancy's eye. She was a blue tortie, much smaller than her peers. But she had the look, the full cheeks, the round muzzle and a sweet and appealing air.

General Description and Judging

The British Shorthair is a medium to large, sturdy cat with a semi-cobby body—a rather short, powerful body—with a full, broad chest, broad shoulders and hips, short, strong, substantial legs, rounded paws and a thick tail. The head is broad and round with a firm

British Shorthair Blue ♂ 1·09

British Shorthair Head: broad; rounded; snub nose; stop; full cheeks. Ears: medium; wide set. Eyes: large; round; wide set. Body: semi-cobby. Coat: short; plush.

chin. The round full cheeks give the cat a chubby, chipmunk appearance. Its eyes should be large, round and expressive. The ears are medium in size, round and set wide apart. The broad nose is short and snub with an obvious change of direction from the bridge. If it is properly proportioned, you should be able to "cup" the head in two areas: the skull and the muzzle should fit into a circular shape.

The fur is short, dense, firm, crisp, well-bodied, with a natural protective appearance. The coat feels like a plush rug and should tingle the hands. It is a pleasure to run your fingers through it. Brindled fur is desirable in all torties in this breed.

Temperament

British Shorthairs are very independent, yet extremely affectionate. They are very alert and quizzical and enjoy following you around the house to make sure you do things right. The males, in particular, are extremely people-oriented, usually downright mushy. This is an extremely quiet, little talking, no-nonsense, "I can take everything in stride" breed of cat. British Shorthairs are easy to groom, as their fur does not tangle and should be combed very lightly. They make ideal pets for less active people as well as for busy households.

British Shorthair White ♂ 1•10

Burmese/Bombay

The Burmese is the gold-eyed sepia beauty of cat fancy. The Bombay is the black panther of cat fancy, with its patent leather coat and copper penny eyes.

Burmese Sable ♂ 5·00

Origin

All contemporary Burmese cats trace their ancestry to a Tonkinese, Wong Mau, brought to the United States in 1930 by Dr. J. Thompson. Dr. Thompson was interested in the unique color of Wong Mau, and, in order to explore it, bred her to a seal point Siamese. The resulting kittens were Siamese, and Tonkinese. The Tonkinese resulting from this breeding, if bred together, or, one of the Tonkinese males bred back to Wong Mau, produced the following kittens: one sepia color, two mink and

one pointed. Such was the start of the Burmese breed as we know it today.

The early Burmese were different from today's, having longer heads and bodies and finer bones. In 1947, the Cat Fancier's Association stopped recognizing the Burmese for championship status because they were not descended from three generations of "Burmese." It was not until 1953 that they were once again allowed championship status. The semi-foreign type of the Burmese of the 1950s remained until the early 1960s, when breeders

started changing the type to the shorter, cobby Burmese seen today.

General Description and Judging

At present the Burmese are bred to be cobby cats with short muzzles and a nose break. Some breeders are working with the red gene by bringing the Burmese of Europe into the United States. The introduction of the red gene into the gene pool will bring cream and all of the torties. The red sepia is tangerine in color and quite beautiful; sepia cream is a tan cream.

Burmese Sable

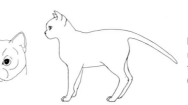

Burmese Head: round; slight break. Ears: medium; wide set. Eyes: large; round; yellow to gold. Body: semi-cobby. Coat: shorthair. Color: eumelanin sepia solid.

able in apartment life as they are in country living. These cats are extremely calm. The breed as a whole is rather quiet in voice. They are easy to care for, needing only an occasional grooming with a fine-tooth comb, and, even better, a rubdown from their owner's hand, which they love. They make excellent pets, and are loyal and affectionate.

Burmese Chocolate ♀ 1·00

The Burmese is a pointed cat. The point color is not easily seen on the sable, except in strong light, but is more readily seen on the other colors. In some organizations, sable may be the only recognized color. In TICA, the Burmese is recognized in sable, blue sepia, chocolate sepia and frost sepia.

The overall impression of the ideal Burmese is a cat of medium size, substantial bone structure, good muscular development and a surprising weight for its size. This, together with its expressive eyes and sweet face, presents a very distinctive cat, comparable to no other breed. Everything about the Burmese is round. The head should be rounded without flat planes: a rounded forehead and a full face with a round short muzzle. There should be considerable breadth between the round, yellow-to-gold eyes. In profile there should be a visible break in the line of the nose. The medium-sized ears are set well apart.

The cobby body should be muscular with a well-developed chest. The legs

are of medium length and boning, with sturdy musculature. The medium-length tail should not be whippy. The close-lying, short coat should be fine, glossy and satin-like in texture.

Temperament

The Burmese are well-known for their great adaptability. They are as comfort-

Burmese Cream ♂ 1·00

Bombay Head: round; slight stop. Ears: medium; wide set. Eyes: large; round; wide set; copper. Body: semi-cobby. Coat: shorthair. Color: solid black.

Bombay

Origin

The Bombay, a man-made breed, was created by breeding a Burmese to a black American Shorthair in 1958. It was not given championship status until 1976. Bombays are often referred to as the small black panthers of the cat fancy world, with their black shining coats and large, round, glowing copper eyes. Black is the only accepted color. Bombays carrying the sepia gene may produce sepia kittens. In TICA these sepia kittens are shown with the Burmese.

In TICA the Bombay is not a black Burmese. The Bombay resembles a moderate Burmese in type; the body and legs may be slightly longer. In profile there should be a moderate stop in the line of the nose. The body is semi-cobby. The tail should be neither long nor whippy. The mature specimen (at four years) should be black to the roots.

Bombay ♂ 1·06

Bombay ♀ 0·05

Temperament

The Bombays have excellent appetites and are healthy cats. They have a sweet disposition, and are rather mellow. They make excellent, loving pets.

Bombay ♂ 0·11

Chartreux

The shorthair natural breed of France. Sometimes called the Monastery Cat or the Blue Cat of France, this copper-eyed blue cat contrasts a large, robust body with rather delicate legs. The Chartreux is also called the Smiling Cat.

Origin

The Chartreux is thought to be one of the most ancient breeds; reference was made to this cat as long ago as 1558. They were reportedly bred by the French Carthusian-Chartreux monks who were also known for their green liqueur, Chartreuse. They were first imported to North America in 1970.

The Chartreux is a sturdy breed known for its hunting ability and for its dense, woolly, water-repellent fur. The medium-short coat is so dense it "breaks" or parts like the wool of a sheep. At one time, the Chartreux were bred as much for their coats as for their hunting ability. Years ago these cats were nearly eliminated because of their rich coats, as the pelts were highly valued in fur trading.

By the 1920s there were very few Chartreux left in France and they were in grave danger of extinction. It was at this time that two French women took an interest in preserving the breed and started a Chartreux breeding program. Within thirteen years their efforts began to pay off when one of their cats became an International Champion in Paris.

The Chartreux, like so many other European breeds, faced near-extinction once again during World War II. Breeders were forced to use Persians and British Shorthairs as mates for their Chartreux in hopes of preserving the bloodlines. In 1950 the Paris Cat Club put a stop to this hybridization and ordered that only Chartreux to Chartreux breeding would be accepted.

General Description and Judging

Its husky, robust type is sometimes termed "primitive," meaning it has gone unchanged from the very beginning. Because of its strong body and

Chartreux ♀ 0·08

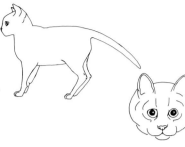

Chartreux Head: broad; round; slight stop permitted; full cheeks. Ears: medium; set high. Eyes: large; round; copper. Body: semi-cobby. Legs: fine-boned. Coat: medium; dense. Color: solid blue.

Temperament

Unfortunately, there are not many Chartreux in France or in the United States today, though they have qualities, such as a certain silent pride and a quiet reserve of energy, that make them outstanding in the show ring and as pets.

Their eyes, the eyes of a survivor, reveal caution and an acute interest in their surroundings. The cat is mellow, taking things in stride while also being alert for any changes that might affect its well-being.

These cats are prepared to meet the challenges of everyday life, and are comfortable with apartment living or country living. They display qualities of strength, intelligence and amenability that have enabled them to survive for centuries without the help of human beings. They are large cats yet they are extremely supple and agile. While

♂ 2·07

short, slender legs, the Chartreux is a swift and deadly hunter.

If one word were to be used to describe the Chartreux, it would be "impressive." It is a solid, healthy, hardy, massive cat, with a smile on its face and huge, expressive, haunting copper eyes. The large head is broad with a high forehead and rounded contours. The jaw is powerful and the cheeks are full. The muzzle is relatively small for the size of the head and helps to give the Chartreux a "smiling" look. The medium-sized nose is straight in pro-

file with a slight stop permitted. The medium to small ears are placed high on the head, rather close together.

The large body is medium-long and sturdy, with strong bones and dense, solid muscles, with broad shoulders and a deep, massive chest and a heavy tail. The legs are medium-short in length and fine-boned, ending with dainty feet.

Any shade of blue is acceptable for the coat, although a silver sheen is desirable. Eye color is gold or copper; copper is preferred.

being "survival" cats, they are perhaps the most nonaggressive of all the breeds. They seem to be able to tolerate any situation and are happy with most surroundings as long as they have human companionship. They make excellent pets, having almost dog-like affection and devotion, and, like the dog, they can be trained to walk on a leash. They have a chirping, rather quiet sound, like that of a bird, rather than the normal meow of cats. All of these qualities make the Chartreux a unique and loving pet.

Cornish Rex

The Cornish Rex is the greyhound of the cat world. The soft, wavy, marcelled coat is unlike that on any other cat. Everything is curly, even the whiskers.

Origin

The first known Rex was born in 1950 in a litter of kittens from two ordinary short-coated cats in Cornwall, England. The coat was different in that it was wavy. The red and white wavy-coated male kitten (named Killibunker) was bred back to its mother, who produced more wavy-coated kittens. These were later to be called Rex, after the rabbits of the same name. All Cornish Rex cats thus trace their ancestry back to Killibunker.

Further breeding revealed the wavy coat to be a true, recessive mutation. Many breeds were used in the development of the Rex, resulting in a large gene pool making almost every color and pattern available.

Cornish Rex Head: oval; Roman profile (slight stop permitted); prominent bridge; definite muzzle break. Ears: large; set high. Eyes: medium; oval. Body: oriental; tuck-up. Coat: wavy; shorthair.

Cornish Rex Tortoiseshell and White ♀ 0·07

Cornish Rex Red Mackerel Tabby ♂ 0·06

Cornish Rex Chocolate Smoke ♀ 0·08

Devon Rex

In 1960, in Devon, England, a similarly coated kitten appeared. At first it was thought that this strain could be used as an outcross for the Cornish Rex but the Devon gene was not compatible with the Cornish Rex gene. When a Cornish was mated to a Devon, only straighthaired kittens were produced. The mutations were located at different positions on the chromosome. The Cornish Rex and the Devon Rex would then go their separate ways, each being bred for different body types and waviness.

General Description and Judging

The Cornish Rex is a foreign typed cat; everything is long and slender. It is considered by many judges and breeders to be the most extreme of all the shorthair cats.

The skull is egg-shaped; the back part of the skull is well-rounded to accentuate the oval-shaped head, which is longer than it is wide. There should be a whisker break. The Cornish Rex has a Roman profile, a slight arch from the forehead to the tip of the nose; there may be a slight change of direction at the eyes, creating two convex curves instead of one continuous downward arch. The striking, often outlandishly large ears have a deep conical appearance and are set high on the head. The eyes are medium in size and oval in shape, set an eye's width apart and are slanted very slightly.

The Cornish has extremely fine boning and stands high on its legs. These cats are sometimes called "spiders" due to their fine boning, yet they feel much heavier than they look and must have substantial hips. The cat must be hard and muscular with no indication of being overly fat or thin. The long body is small to medium in size; the rib cage is full and deep, and the backbone follows an upward curve forming a "tuck up" like that of a greyhound. The tail is long and thin. The feet are small and oval.

The coat displays deep, even waves; waves that extend to the head, legs and tail are more desirable. The coat is short, fine, very soft and dense. The cat is a delight to feel, the hair so soft and wavy that it feels like velvet ripples in your hand. The Cornish Rex is recognized in all colors of all divisions.

Cornish Rex Parti-Color Point ♀ 0•07

Cornish Rex
Tortoiseshell and White ♀ 0·04

much hair to protect it from the cold. Although it has a normal temperature, the Rex may feel warmer than other cats.

Rex cats are extremely curious about their surroundings. They indulge in special acrobatics and "ground speed racing" and are known to be clowns. Their easy grooming, soft wavy coat and intelligence make them delightful cats to show and to have as pets.

Temperament

The Cornish Rex has a very alert and athletic look and is very intelligent, outgoing and affectionate. Little or no grooming is required, as the cat does not constantly shed. But one of the greatest delights is hand grooming the Rex; to run your hand over the body of a Rex feels so pleasant that care must be taken to not overdo it. This cat likes a warmer environment, as there is not

Cornish Rex
Tortoiseshell ♀ 0·09

Devon Rex

Its huge, low-set, batlike ears and large, oval-shaped eyes make the Devon Rex the pixie or elf of Cat Fancy. The Devon has wavy hair, but it is not "marcelled" like the Cornish Rex.

Origin

The Devon Rex appeared in 1960 in Devon, England. At first breeders tried to breed the Devon to the Cornish Rex. This proved to be of no advantage. The resulting kittens had straight hair and presented no improvement in type. Breeders introduced other breeds into their gene pool, but these early outcrosses did not produce the desired type. Outcrossing was then done only when necessary for the health and coat density of the breed. The Devon gene produces Devon type; in second generation kittens, plain coated kittens are of domestic type, but the curlies all have Devon type.

Devon Rex Black ♀ 3·06

*Devon Rex
Brown Mackerel Tabby*
♂ 0·06

General Description and Judging

The Devon's body is slender and of medium length and frame, with a long neck and a hard, muscular, broad chest. Long, slim legs carry the body high off the ground. The hind legs are higher than the front legs. The long, slender tail should be covered with short fur.

The small head is a modified wedge, with a short muzzle and a series of three distinct convex curves: outer edge of ears, cheekbones and whisker pads. The prominent whisker pads define a good muzzle break. The cheeks are very full. In profile, there should be a definite stop with the forehead curving back to a flat skull. A straight profile is not desirable, as it will not allow the formation of the pronounced muzzle break. The set of the ears is as much on

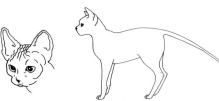

Devon Rex Head: modified wedge; stop; muzzle break; full cheeks. Ears: large; low set. Eyes: large; oval. Body: semi-foreign. Coat: wavy; shorthair.

Temperament

The Devon is alert, active and shows a lively interest in its surroundings. It has a good disposition, a very quiet voice and is especially suitable for apartment life. These cats make sweet, loving pets and are a delight to show.

Devon Rex White ♂ 0·08

the side as on the top of the head. The ears are ridiculously large, adding to the elfin look. The large, oval eyes are set wide apart.

The coat is very short and soft with a relaxed wave, feeling like suede. Whiskers and eyebrows are crinkled. Some Devons even have ear tufts and ear muffs (a patch of fur on the outside lower part of the ear) that accentuate their pixie look. The full-bodied yet fine, short, wavy fur that covers the Devon is of a distinctive texture because of the rexing of the Devon gene. No other recognized breed has this mutation. Devons may have down on the underparts of the body; this is not bareness. The coat may be thinner than that of the Cornish Rex. Allowances may be made for lack of full coat development on kittens with very good type, over fully coated kittens of a lesser type.

Devon Rex Blue

Egyptian Mau

The gooseberry-green-eyed Mau is the only natural spotted domestic cat. It may be descended from the small African wild cat, *Felis libyca*. The Mau, whose name means "cat" in Egyptian, is a very rare breed.

Origin

The Mau closely resembles the cats in the wall paintings of ancient Egypt; its ancestors could have been the cat loved and worshiped in those times.

The modern Mau reportedly dates back to 1953 in Italy. There, the Princess Natalie Troubetskoy saw a Mau, a smoke tabby male, for the first time. She fell in love with this unique cat, and persuaded the owner, the Egyptian ambassador to Italy, to help her obtain a kitten from Cairo. This was a silver female named Baba. The ambassador bred his cat with the hope of producing another Mau kitten; the bronze tabby male kitten was bred back to its mother, producing a female who was given the name Lisa. Exhibition of these cats took place in 1955, at the Rome Cat Show. English cat fanciers at that show wanted to be able to produce Egyptian Maus in Britain. They were to attempt this by using Abyssinians, Siamese, and tabbies. These hybrids, however, did not resemble the original Maus.

In 1956, the Princess traveled to the United States with her three Maus. Shown for the first time in the United States the following year, Baba became the first champion Mau.

The Maus in the United States are reportedly descended from Baba, and not from the British hybrids. The Egyptian Maus, however, have a "scarab" shape on the forehead; Maus in the United States do not, but have a characteristic "M" mark on the forehead. A different report claims that the first pair of Maus, named Gepa and Ludol, came to the United States in 1953. The Mau had to wait until 1968 for championship recognition in some organizations. The first true Mau brought to Britain from Egypt arrived in 1978.

Egyptian Mau Head: modified wedge; rounded contours. Ears: medium; set back. Eyes: large; oval; light green. Body: semi-foreign. Coat: shorthair. Pattern: spotted tabby. Colors: silver, bronze, or black smoke.

Egyptian Mau Silver ♀ 0·06

General Description and Judging

The old Mau standard is very similar (except for tabby pattern and colors) to the Abyssinian. In TICA, the new standard reflects the "realistic" Mau. The Mau is definitely not a spotted Abyssinian. The body is not a foreign type but a cross between the foreign and cobby. The eyes are a round almond shape. The ears are medium to medium-large.

The rare Egyptian Mau is shown in three spotted color patterns: bronze (brown spotted), silver (black silver spotted) and smoke (black smoke tabby).

The head is a rounded, modified wedge shape, with a medium-sized, rounded muzzle and a slight stop to the line of the nose. The medium to large ears are placed well back on the head. The large, almond-shaped eyes are gooseberry green. The facial expression is that of "I didn't do it!" or one of surprise.

The semi-foreign, medium-long body shows well-developed musculature and medium boning. The hind legs are longer than the front legs. The high-set shoulder blades, higher than most breeds, give the Mau a cheetah-like gait. The Mau is equipped with a "belly flap" which allows the hind legs to stretch out a considerable distance, making it a very swift runner.

The medium-length coat is silky, fine and resilient. The cat's spotted pattern and its light green eyes give it a beautiful, wild look. It is said that the baby teeth of a Mau kitten do not fall out until the adult teeth have come in, making it possible for a young Mau to have two sets of teeth at once.

Egyptian Mau
Black Smoke ♂ 1•05

Egyptian Mau Bronze
♂ 1•01

Temperament

Egyptian Maus are active, colorful cats, curious about everything, yet reserved. They love to lap sit or ride on their owner's shoulders. They have been known to "cup" their paws like hands to drink water. They are quite friendly and affectionate to the people they like but will sometimes shy away from strangers. When the Mau is happy, it may wag its tail like a dog. The mother and the father cats will both take care of the kittens. Maus make delightful pets.

Havana

Some cat fanciers believe that these unique reddish brown cats with green eyes originated in Siam, where they were kept to protect their owners from evil. Others acknowledge the Havana as a man-made breed developed in England in the 1950s.

Origin

The earlier modern Havana cats were a reddish brown chocolate color, a color so beautiful that it challenged early breeders to see if it could be purposely reproduced. In the early 1950s, British breeders started working together to produce this particular shade of chocolate.

The first kitten born with the desired color was a cross between a seal point Siamese (carrying chocolate) and a shorthaired black. The black was an offspring of a seal point Siamese bred to a black cat. The possible colors from this breeding would be: two blacks, two chocolate points, two solid chocolates and two seal points. The two solid chocolates may be the foundation of the new breed as it is known today.

The brown is a rich reddish brown, a deeper cinnamon brown color or a mahogany brown. It is not a black brown. It is speculated that a modifier may be present, changing the dark brown to reddish brown.

The early Havanas also had Russian Blue in their background. This makes it possible for the maltesing gene (d/d) to be carried recessively in the chocolates (b/b, d/d). It is a genetic possibility to have a frost in a brown litter. The frost, a warm taupe color with a rosy cast, is a recognized color in some organizations.

Type in the early Havanas looked very much like that of the compact Burmese, and was criticized for not being unique. The color was established, but, in England, no one could agree what the Havana type should look like. In 1958 the Governing Council of Cat Fanciers recognized the Havana as a Chestnut Brown Foreign Shorthair. In 1959 the type and standard changed to be more in line with the Russian Blue standard.

Only in the United States has the breed reached the distinction of being unique. In the mid-1950s a pair of Havanas was taken to the United States, and from then on the breed was developed until it no longer resembled the European Burmese or the chocolate

Havana Chocolate ♂ 1·07

Oriental Shorthair. The Havana in America today presents a striking contrast between the rich chocolate and the green eyes, yet the cat is not extreme in any fashion.

This is still a rare breed, even in the United States, as there are not very many Havana breeders.

General Description and Judging

This is a breed of moderate type with the exception of the long legs and large ears. The head is a modified wedge with rounded contours, longer than it is wide with a definite, exaggerated stop, so pronounced that it appears to be scooped out. This stop and muzzle break are trademarks of the Havana. The strong muzzle is almost square. The large ears, though not close-set, give the animal a very alert look. The large oval eyes should not be so large that they appear to bulge.

The medium-sized body is of semi-foreign type, with a slender, medium-length tail. The legs should be long for the size of the cat, and slender but not thin. The smooth, short coat has a glossy sheen. The frosts, because of the maltesing gene, may have fuller, less smooth, less soft coats than the chocolates.

Temperament

Havanas are highly intelligent cats who truly enjoy being around people. They are not as vocal as Siamese, nor are they as aggressive. They make affectionate pets and lovely show cats.

Havana Frost ♀ 0•09

Havana Head: modified wedge; definite stop and muzzle break; rounded contours. Ears: large; wide set. Eyes: large; oval; green. Body: semi-foreign. Coat: shorthair. Colors: solid chocolate and frost.

Havana Chocolate

Japanese Bobtail

The long, elegant cat with a pom-pom tail, the Japanese Bobtail is a very old breed in Japan, known and loved for its clear, "painted-on" good luck *Mi-Ke* pattern.

Origin

Manuscripts, paintings and other Japanese works of art give evidence that the Bobtail existed in Japan at least a thousand years ago. The unique markings of the cat were shown, though often with no mention of the short kinked tail. The Mi-Ke cat may still be seen on the Gotokuji Temple in Tokyo and as the "sleeping cat" on the Niko Temple.

In 1968 the first pair of Japanese Bobtails arrived in the United States. They were sent to Elizabeth Freret in Virginia by Judy Crawford, an American who had been raising them for about fifteen years while living in Ja-

Japanese Bobtail
Black and White ♂ 2·01

Japanese Bobtail Head: wedge; gentle contours; high cheekbones; muzzle break; slight stop. Ears: large; wide set. Eyes: large; oval. Body: foreign. Coat: shorthair.

pan. The first litter of kittens was born the following year. Mrs. Crawford later returned to the United States and continued her interest in breeding Bobtails.

In 1970 the International Japanese Bobtail Fancier's Association was formed. There are still many Bobtails in Japan, but they are, for the most part, household pets and are not exhibited in the championship class. Most Bobtails in Japan have the Mi-Ke pattern; some are one color and white.

The usual Mi-Ke color pattern of the Bobtail is the same as the calico (for females), a good luck three-color combination of red, black and white. Other typical combinations would be black and white or red and white.

General Description and Judging

The tail of the Japanese Bobtail is unlike that of any other cat. If it could be pulled out to its full length, it would measure four to five inches long; it appears to be about two inches long when curled close to the body. When the cat is relaxed, the tail may be carried in an upright position. The tailbone is usually strong and rigid rather than jointed (except at the base) and is composed of one or several curves and angles. The hair on the tail is somewhat longer and thicker than the body hair. This creates the pom-pom or bunny tail effect, which appears to commence at the base of the spine and camouflages the underlying bone structure of the

tail. The gene causing the pom-pom tail is not related to the Manx gene. The Japanese Bobtail carries none of the lethal genes that affect the Manx.

Another feature is the unique set of the cat's eyes, combined with very high cheekbones and a long parallel nose. The large ears are set wide apart, as are the large, oval eyes, which are set into the skull at a rather pronounced slant. This gives the cat a distinctive look unlike other oriental breeds. The eyeball shows a shallow curvature and should not bulge out beyond the cheekbone or forehead. The head is a modified wedge with long, finely chiseled but gently curving lines; it should fit into an almost perfect equilateral triangle. The long nose has a gentle dip at

Japanese Bobtail Brown Mackerel Tabby and White ♂ 4·04

or just below eye level. The muzzle is broad and rounded; there should be a definite muzzle break.

The body is of foreign type. This is a medium-sized cat, with long, clean lines and bone structure. It is well-muscled, yet rather slender in build. The hind legs are noticeably longer than the forelegs. When standing, the cat's forelegs and shoulders form two uninterrupted straight lines.

The coat is medium in length, and very soft and silky in texture. There should be only a slight undercoat, causing the hair to lie close to the body.

White Spotting Gene

The white spotting gene (S/-) is seen in its clearest, most definite patterns on the Japanese Bobtail. The tortie and white female is especially splendid. The black and red are of intense color. One theory is that the white spotting gene serves as a gate or fence, holding the color in one place. The pigment may be of thick or dense deposit, making the color a deeper intensity; the colors may also appear to be darker because they are surrounded by brilliant white. There may be no melanophores in the epidermis of the white spotted areas.

If the cat is of classic, mackerel or spotted tabby pattern, this pattern will be evident in the phaeomelanin patches. These cats are not patched tabbies or torbies, as the eumelanin is not tabbied.

It is possible for any of the cats with the Mi-Ke pattern to have blue or odd eyes. The migration of embryonic tissue may be affected by the white spotting gene; migration of neural crest cells to the iris takes place shortly after birth. Pigmentation does not take place until this migration occurs. If the white spotting gene extends to or over one eye or both eyes, no pigment is deposited. The light goes into the eye and is reflected out, making the eye appear blue.

It is not uncommon for the ear on the blue side to be hearing impaired or completely deaf, as the development of the ear may also be affected if the white spotting gene is present. The ear is formed but the hearing mechanism is not completely formed because cell migration is not continued. The nerves connecting the hearing organs to the brain are simply not completed, and the cat is incapable of hearing.

Temperament

Japanese Bobtails are intelligent and charming; they love to play and make excellent companions. People who have these cats would not think of owning another breed. Little grooming is required, as they do not shed. One of the noticeable characteristics of the Japanese Bobtails is their clannish nature: they have very strong family ties. Mother cats will continue to take care of their kittens long after they reach adulthood. Family groups remain as a unit, playing and sleeping together. They are a very quiet breed, and will usually speak only when spoken to.

Japanese Bobtail Tortoiseshell and White ♀ 0·05

*Japanese Bobtail
Tortoiseshell and White* ♀ 1·02

Korat

The Korat, rare in the United States, is the silver-blue good luck cat with huge, green eyes. The heart-shaped head of the Korat is like that of no other breed.

Origin

This is a very old shorthair breed from Thailand, dating back as far as the mid-fourteenth century. The Korat was first seen in England at a cat show as early as 1896. The first pair to be imported to the United States arrived in 1959 and were registered at that time. In 1966 the Korat competed in the championship classes for the first time. By 1969 all associations in North America recognized them for championship.

Many believe the Korat to be the forerunner of the blue point Siamese. In Thailand, the Korats are known as Si-Sawat cats. *Si* means color. *Sawat* means good fortune or prosperity; it also means a mingled color of gray and light green.

The Thais consider these cats to be symbols of good fortune; their silvery blue color signifies wealth. The gift of a pair of Si-Sawat cats to a bride insures a fortunate marriage. The Thai people place so much value on the Si-Sawat cat that it is rare for one to be sold. They will give them as gifts to those they hold in high esteem.

General Description and Judging

This is a semi-cobby, shorthair cat of great strength, with a pale, silvery blue coat, a heart-shaped face and large, luminous green eyes. The expressive eyes are unlike those of other cats; they are oversized for the face, with great depth and an intense gaze. The eyes must be set well apart, fitting into the wide top part of the heart shape of the face or the "look" of the Korat is not there. An amber cast to the green eyes is acceptable.

One of the most distinctive aspects of this breed is the double-heart-shaped head: a heart-shaped face on a heart-shaped head. The eyebrow ridges form the upper curves, which run gently down to the muzzle to complete the heart. The forehead is large and flat. The large ears are set high on the head. There is a slight stop between the forehead and nose.

Korat ♀ 1·07

The semi-cobby body is of medium size, muscular, with strong leg boning, giving a sense of the power of a hard-coiled spring and unexpected weight for its size. The back is carried in a curve. The tail is medium in length. The legs are of moderate length, the front legs slightly shorter than the back legs.

The single coat is short to medium in length, glossy and fine, lying close to the body. The color is pale silver-blue all over, with no shading or tabby markings. The silver tipping gives a frosty or silvery sheen or halo effect over the entire cat, like a silver cloud over a blue sky.

Temperament

Korats are very intelligent and make loving pets. They are very quiet, having a very soft voice. It is to be remembered that the Korats are very slow to develop and go through an "ugly duckling" stage when they are young. Korats have a keen sense of hearing, sight and scent. They are very gentle, moving softly with caution, disliking sudden, loud or harsh noises. They form a very strong bond with their owner and truly enjoy being near the ones they love, making loyal and delightful pets.

Korat Head: heart-shaped face and head; flat forehead; slight stop. Ears: large; set high. Eyes: large; wide set; green. Body: semi-cobby. Coat: shorthair. Color: solid silver-blue.

Korat ♀ 0·10

Korat

Maine Coon

The Maine Coon, one of the largest among breeds of domestic cats, is often referred to as the gentle giant of cat fancy. It is lynx-like in appearance, yet gentle in temperament. It is North America's only natural longhair breed, and the state of Maine's official cat.

Origin

The Maine Coon's origin is not known. Many believe the Norwegian Forest Cat to be an ancestor of the Maine Coon; indeed, some of the present-day Norwegian Forest Cats in Norway resemble the Maine Coon. Others believed them to be the result of matings, in Maine, between semi-wild domestic cats and raccoons (a genetic impossibility), hence the name. Another story tells that a cat was brought by ship to Maine by a certain Captain Coon, and that it escaped, lived in the woods and mated with the semi-wild domestic cats. The breed probably developed through a process of natural selection. Whatever the origin, it may be surmised that breeders discovered these wonderful animals and carefully bred them to preserve the look of the original "wild" Maine Coons.

There is little doubt that this breed has been around for a long time. Maine Coons were exhibited in many of the early cat shows, one winning at the 1895 Madison Square Garden Cat Show. These magnificent cats fell from

Maine Coon Silver
Mackerel Tabby
♂ 1·07

Maine Coon Head: broad; modified wedge; rounded contours; high cheekbones; square muzzle. Ears: large; set high. Eyes: large; oval. Body: long; substantial. Coat: semi-longhair; uneven.

favor with the arrival of the flashier Persians from Great Britain, only to come back to full glory in recent years through the dedicated efforts of American breeders.

The earlier Maine Coons were often regarded with disdain, some breeders referring to them as barn cats or alley cats. They did not have an eye for the rugged beauty of this cat! In the 1950s Maine Coons were shown once again and in the 1970s they started making a real comeback by winning Best in Show awards. The Maines of today hold their own with any other breeds. In the past, judges had been reluctant to award these rugged-looking, unpolished cats, so different from the manicured, every-hair-in-place, magnificent Persians. In today's cat shows, Maines may outnumber some of the other breeds. The Maines are here to stay!

General Description and Judging

The Maine Coon is a mixture of elegance and ruggedness, wildness and gentleness. It is a large, semi-long-haired cat, with a shaggy coat, large ears and an extremely long, full, plume tail; a "working" cat, able to fend for itself in rough, woody terrain and under extreme climate conditions, exhibiting exceptional strength due to heavy boning and sturdy muscles.

Maines are very slow to mature, not reaching full growth until three to five years of age. Males weigh twelve to eighteen pounds; females may be smaller. The Maine, however, should not be judged on poundage and size alone. Without the large ears, high cheekbones, strong, square muzzle, the long, strong, rectangular body, firm legs and large paws, and the extra-long, bushy tail, the "look" is not there. The head shape is a broad modified wedge, with rounded contours, wide nose and a square muzzle. The strikingly large, wide ears are set well apart on top of the head, never on the sides, and should not flare out. Lynx tipping and ear furnishings are desirable. The eyes are large and oval. Legs should be of medium length. The tail should be the same length as the measure from the base of the neck to the base of the spine. The shaggy, uneven coat lies flat, having very little undercoat. Toe tufts may be present, which, some believe, aides the cat in walking on snow. Maine Coons may be shown in all colors and patterns except the pointed, sepia and mink colors.

Maine Coon Blue Classic Tabby ♂ 0·08

Maine Coon Brown Classic Tabby   ♀ 0·05

Habits

Tail cleaning is an accomplishment, due to the length of the tail and body. Sometimes the cat wraps the tail around a front leg and proceeds to clean it in a spiral motion. Some Maines use their front paws like hands. Their curled front claws and toes are a little longer than those of the average cat, enabling them to pick up and hold slim objects such as pencils. Front feet are also used to pick at food, taking a small piece and dropping it on the floor to eat. If given a piece of meat, it must be "killed," then washed by dunking in water before eating. Maines love to put both front legs in the water dish before drinking and even relish a deep drinking container for deeper water standing.

Temperament

Males tend to be very possessive of their owner and extremely loyal. Females may appear, at times, to be grumpy, especially if they can bluff you. They may first growl; if that doesn't work, they will "huff and puff." Even a small kitten can call this bluff, causing the twelve pounder to slink away with tail between its legs. The females are excellent mothers, which is just as well, as litters may number seven or eight kittens.

Maines are extremely intelligent and exhibit a keen interest in their surroundings. These are mellow cats, amiable and easy to get along with when they know you. They give the impression of being kind and considerate. They do not necessarily want to be held, but want to be close to the person they love, following from room to room. Usually they will bond with only one person and are completely loyal to that individual. They are usually very quiet, although when they see something as interesting as a bug or a bird, they may stand on their hind legs, like a bear, and make a chirping sound. Many Maines will fetch and return an object. They do not like to be restricted, yet, loving the outdoors, they can be trained to walk on a leash. They enjoy the snow and seem to even enjoy getting wet. These are truly the gentle giants; they own you, not the other way around.

◄ *Maine Coon Brown Classic Tabby*

Maine Coon Brown Classic Tabby ♂ 0•10

Manx/Cymric

The shorthaired Manx and the longhaired Cymric are the only tailless cats in the cat fancy world. These shy cats have a unique, flared ear set. They have a rabbit-like gait due to their cobby body and the height of their hindquarters. They are polite, reserved ladies and gentlemen.

Origin

There are some outlandish stories about how tailless cats came to the Isle of Man, where they may indeed have originated. Some say the Irish brought the cats to the island, using cats' tails as plumes for their helmets. Others say Phoenician traders brought the cats with them from Japan and thus the Manx must be related to the Japanese Bobtail. This cannot be true, in part because the gene causing the curled tail of the Japanese Bobtail is different. In another story, a tailless cat swam ashore from a ship of the Spanish Armada. According to one more story, the cat was aboard Noah's ark and Noah shut a door on the cat's tail, cutting it off.

Taillessness is the result of a dominant gene that occurred long ago. Due to a high death rate among kittens, there is a scarcity of Manx today. Kittens from a homozygous dominant will die during the fetal stage, when the development of the spine is hindered.

Cymric

The Cymric is the longhaired version of the Manx, first appearing in Manx litters in the 1960s. They should have the same conformation as the Manx. The breed is named Cymric (pronounced "kumric") from "Cymru," the Welsh name for Wales. The Cymric did not gain recognition until the 1970s and is still not recognized by all organizations. If there are few Manx today, there are even fewer Cymrics.

General Description and Judging

The key word in describing the Manx or Cymric is round: round head, round chest and round rump. The overall appearance should be that of a medium-

Manx Head: round; slight stop; definite muzzle break; full cheeks. Ears: medium; wide set. Eyes: large; round. Body: cobby. Appears tailless. Coat: short; double.

Manx White ♂ 6·05

Manx Brown Classic Tabby ♂ 1·10

Cymric Head: round; slight stop; definite muzzle break; large, round whisker pads; full cheeks. Ears: medium; wide set. Eyes: large; round. Body: cobby; substantial. Appears tailless. Coat: semi-longhair; double.

Cymric Red Mackerel Tabby ♂ 1·00

sized, compact, muscular cat having the look of a bear with no tail. The head is slightly longer than broad, with a gentle curve below the bridge. The broad muzzle is slightly longer than wide, with a definite muzzle break and large, round whisker pads. The cheekbones should be prominent; there should be jowls, especially in adult males. The placement of the medium-sized ears is very important: they must be set wide apart, so that when viewed from behind they flair out to resemble the rockers of a cradle. The eyes are round, large and full.

The medium-sized body is cobby, with sturdy boning, and is well-muscled, including the legs, giving a robust, stout appearance. The hind legs are higher than the front legs. The short back forms a smooth, uninterrupted arch from the shoulders to the rump, curving at the rump to form the desired round look. There should be great depth of flank, adding to the cobby appearance. Taillessness must be absolute in the perfect specimen. The Manx has a short, soft, plush, double coat. The double coat of the Cymric is semi-longhaired, fine and silky.

Temperament

Once the kittens are past the endangered stage of development, they grow to be strong, healthy adults. The Manx make excellent pets. They do tend to be loyal to only one person and aloof but not unkind to others. They are excellent hunters and enjoy tree climbing. They are quiet, rather reserved cats and are excellent, faithful companions especially for the person living alone.

Manx Black and White ♂ 0·11

Norwegian Forest Cat

The native longhaired cat of Norway. It has a thick, heavy, all-weather coat, a huge, bushy tail and large, appealing, almond-shaped eyes. These strong, sturdy, intelligent cats like to walk beside you like a loving dog.

Norwegian Forest Cat
Brown Classic Tabby ♀ 6·01

Origin

The Norwegian Forest Cat, or Skogkatt, is a very old breed in Norway; their origin is unknown. The Norwegians say they have been around forever. They are not of Persian descent, as Persian cats did not enter Norway until the twentieth century and the Forest Cat dates back much earlier. It is not a domesticated wild cat; zoologists agree that Scandinavia had no wild cats.

In Norway, the early Forest Cat lived outdoors, and they still prefer to be outdoors. Norse mythology speaks of a cat so huge that even the god Thor could not lift it from the ground. The goddess of love and fertility, Freya, had a carriage pulled by two large cats.

Forest Cats developed the necessary attributes for survival: a heavy, double coat; sturdy boning; long hind legs and strong claws for swift, strong running, jumping and climbing, enhancing their hunting ability and allowing them to be comfortable on the snow, in a tree, or in rocky terrain. In earlier days thousands of these cats

lived in the wooded areas of the Norwegian countryside. Through the years they became more and more rare until they were on the verge of disappearing as a separate breed. It was not until the early 1970s that a real effort was made to preserve this unique breed. There are over twelve hundred presently registered in Norway. They are fairly new to the United States; the first breeding pair was exported in 1979, and the first surviving litter was born in 1981. The breed' was recognized for championship status in TICA in 1984.

The coloring of some of the Norwegians in Norway is black smoke and white. American cat fanciers who recently went to Norway reported that the Forest Cats there are larger than most in the United States, and noted that the Norwegian cats resemble the Maine Coons in America.

*Norwegian Forest Cat
Brown Mackerel Tabby
and White ♂ 0·09*

Norwegian Forest Cat Head: wedge;
straight lines. Ears: medium-large. Eyes:
large; almond. Body: medium-long;
substantial. Coat: longhair.

General Description and Judging

The body of the Norwegian Forest Cat
is large and imposing, of moderate
length, with heavy boning and substantial musculature. There should be considerable depth of flank. The legs are
medium in length, the hind legs longer
than the forelegs. The full, flowing tail
is as long as the body. The straight lines
of the head should fit into an equilateral

*Norwegian Forest Cat
Brown Classic Tabby and White ♂ 0·11*

triangle. The muzzle is nearly square. The almond-shaped eyes are extremely large and expressive. The ears are medium to large, placed as much on the side as on the top of the head, with ear furnishings extending beyond the outer edge of the ear.

The distinctive all-weather, double coat is semi-long, uneven and dense, with a full ruff. The Norwegian cat seems to enjoy being out in the rain, walking through and playing in mud puddles. Rain water beads up on the top of the coat; bathing can be a problem as it takes a lot of shampoo to cut through the oil in the coat. It is not usually necessary to comb them out as the fur usually does not mat. In general, grooming is no problem; the cats groom themselves and keep themselves very clean.

Temperament

The Norwegian cats have a soothing disposition. Many owners have said that they have had cats all their lives and never have encountered such lovable ones. If the cats have a fault, it is that they want to be with you and love you all the time. But lap sitters they are not, or only on their own terms. They will pile up on your bed at night but prefer not to sleep under the covers. They are gentle yet can be quite firm in having their requirements met. Extremely calm in appearance, they do not miss a thing.

They are usually very quiet, so quiet that it is difficult to know when the female is in season. They usually consider game-playing beneath their dignity, and will sit quietly observing other cats at play. At times, however, there will be a sudden burst of kittenish behavior. They are very intelligent, dependable and sensible. Very good about coming when called, when outdoors they will follow their owner as a dog would, thoroughly enjoying the walk, chasing squirrels and charging up trees. With delight they bring in prizes from the outdoors: a leaf, a live mouse or a small garden snake. They are not picky about their food but some will refuse to eat if deprived of human companionship. Their ancestors were known to eat roots of plants and wasps' nests along with their regular diet of whatever they could catch.

A breeder in Norway said: "The Skogkatt is a very kind, lovable cat, though with the genuine instincts of a cat having to cope with a rough life outdoors. It is in many ways like the real alley cat, only with a long, beautiful coat which requires much less care than that of other longhaired cats . . . From the beginning, nature permitted the survival of only the fittest, and, in the spirit of this principle, the Norwegian Forest Cat emerged from the woodlands of Norway to international recognition. As a result of the extreme conditions of life, this cat naturally gained and manifested its special traits along with intelligence, courage and speed."

Norwegian Forest Cat Silver Mackerel Tabby and White ♂ 0•07

Ocicat

The spotted leopard of cat fancy, the Ocicat is one of the newest recognized breeds, a man-made mix of Abyssinian, Siamese and American Shorthair. It is a large cat with a feral look. Care is given in breeding the Ocicat to perpetuate a loving, sweet disposition.

Origin

The first Ocicat, Tonga, was born in 1964. Her breeder, Virginia Daly, experimenting with a breeding program, wanted to put the agouti tabby pattern on her lynx point Siamese by crossing Abyssinian and Siamese. The first hybrids were all phenotypically Abyssinian. A female hybrid from this cross mated a chocolate point Siamese. Among the offspring was the sought-after agouti lynx point Siamese, and Tonga, who had bright golden spots on an ivory ground color.

Tonga, sold as a pet, was neutered. When other such cats arrived from further matings of Tonga's dam, sire and other relatives, their unique beauty could not be ignored. A serious breeding program for Ocicats began. Mrs. Daly and a few dedicated breeders have worked over the past twenty years to perfect the color, pattern, type and disposition of this cat. Early breeders not only worked with the Abyssinian and Siamese, but introduced the American Shorthair into the gene pool to increase the size of the offspring. This brought in the desired silver gene.

Today, breeders no longer use the Siamese or American Shorthair. Since 1986, only the Abyssinian could be used as an outcross to improve type and enlarge the gene pool. In 1987 the Ocicat was granted championship status in TICA, CFA and the Canadian Cat Association (CCA).

General Description and Judging

The Ocicat is a large, spotted tabby cat of a moderate type, noted for its "wild" appearance. The breeders' intention was to create a cat that captured the distinctive look of a feral spotted cat while preserving the good temperament of the domestic animal. While closest in type to the Abyssinian, the ideal Ocicat is a larger, more robust and athletic animal than today's show quality Abyssinian. The average female weighs seven to ten pounds, the male twelve to fifteen pounds.

The semi-foreign typed body is substantial. The medium-long legs are well-muscled and sturdy; the hind legs are slightly longer than the forelegs. The tail should be long. The head is a modified wedge with rounded contours, with a slight stop from the bridge of the nose to the brow, a good muzzle and a strong chin. The moderately large ears are set on the corners of the

Ocicat Silver Spotted Tabby ♂ 0·06

head; lynx tipping is desirable. The large, almond-shaped eyes are rather wide-set. The fine coat, which should be long enough to carry several bands of ticking, is thick, tight and close-lying.

The pattern of the Ocicat is unique, with large, thumbprint-shaped spots that appear to be randomly scattered across the torso, following the classic tabby markings. The sides never match; each should show a spot circled by spots mimicking the classic tabby "bull's eye." The better Ocicats have spots on the haunches, shoulders, legs and tail and have dorsal spots rather than a stripe. Ocicats are shown only in the spotted tabby pattern and eumelanist colors. Eumelanin may or may not be silvered.

The exact allele or modifier has not been identified for the spotted pattern. There are several theories. One is that the mackerel pattern is incompletely dominant over the classic pattern, causing the pattern to break up into spots. Good spotted patterns may be produced by breeding classic to mack-

Ocicat Silver Spotted Tabby ♂ 0·06

Ocicat Head: modified wedge: rounded contours. Ears: moderately large. Eyes: large; almond. Body: semi-foreign; substantial. Coat: shorthair. Pattern: spotted tabby. Colors: eumelanin.

erel. Some "spotted tabbies" appear to breed true. For this reason, it was thought that there was a spotted gene or a fourth tabby pattern allele; it is not known where this gene would place on the ladder of dominance within the tabby allelic system.

The theory of a separate modifier may hold up the best. It is speculated that this modifier may break up any of the tabby patterns into spots. These spots appear to follow either the mackerel or classic tabby pattern. It is further suggested that this modifier acts as a dominant.

Temperament

Ocicats are loving and gentle and very intelligent. They can be taught to respond to voice commands and seem to enjoy performing tricks. They look like spotted leopards yet have the loving disposition of any domestic pussycat.

The Persian is considered by many to be the aristocrat of cat fancy. It was revered from the first moment it was seen and has held top billing ever since, as it is a glorious combination of flowing coat, muscular strength, small ears, huge, round eyes and, ideally, a sweet expression.

Origin

The Persian, Exotic Shorthair and Himalayan share a common standard and type. The only difference between these breeds is coat length, texture and color. The Persian is a non-pointed longhaired cat; the Exotic Shorthair is a shorthaired Persian in type; the Himalayan is a pointed Persian.

Persians have been shown as a recognized breed for over a hundred years. The exact origin of the Persian is unknown. By some accounts they originated in Asia Minor and were first seen in Europe in the early 1700s, although there were reports of longhaired cats in Italy (imported from Asia) in the late 1500s. Early British books referred to these cats as French cats or Angoras. They were reported to have come from Ankara, Turkey, also the supposed birthplace of the Turkish Angora, to whom they bore a close resemblance. The Turkish Angora was used in many breeding programs as it was prized for its beautiful long coat; it is speculated that Turkish Angora genes can be found in many of our modern cats.

Most of the Persians exhibited at the first cat show in Britain, in 1871, were black, blue or white. Queen Victoria and other members of Britain's royal family kept blue Persians, adding to their popularity. Gradually, different colors and patterns have been introduced and accepted for championship competition, though blue is still a popular color. Persians were first introduced to North America toward the end of the nineteenth century and were just as popular among the breeders, exhibitors and judges in this country as they were in Britain and Asia.

Contemporary, "ideal" show Persians bear little resemblance to their ancestors. The earlier Persians had longer faces, larger ears, smaller, more closely-set eyes and rangier, longer bodies. The type of the early Persian

Persian Cream ♂ 0·11

Persian Blue-eyed Wh ♀ 0·08

alayan

Persian Cream and White ♀ 0·11

Persian Cream and White

was changed radically with the introduction of longhaired cats from Persia (Iran) into the "Angora-Persian" gene pool. The Iranian Persian brought sturdy bodies, short legs, broader, rounder heads and longer, thicker fur. When the Angora and the Iranian cats were crossed, the foreign type began to disappear, and the cobby type replaced the rangier early type. Subsequent cats were bred to capitalize on the sturdy, compact Iranian Persian type. The breed was soon known simply as Persian.

General Description and Judging

The cat should be firm in flesh, not fat, and well-balanced physically and temperamentally, giving the impression of

Persian White ♂ 0·11

Persian Red ♀ 0·11

robust power. The cobby body is well-rounded; the boning is sturdy, large and in proportion to the body. The muscles are firm and well-developed. The back should be short and level. The tail should be short, yet in proportion to the body; the plumed tail of the Persian and Himalayan should be short, carried without a curve at an angle lower than the back, but not trailed when walking. In front view, forelegs should be short and straight, adding to a sturdy appearance, but not with a bulldog look; viewed from behind, the legs should be straight. The chest is to be deep, equally massive across the shoulders and rump with a short, well-rounded midsection. The feet are large and round with short toes; in the longhairs, toe tufts are desirable.

The coat of the Persian and Himalayan should be full of life. The down hairs are dense, making the coat stand off from the body. The hair should be long all over the body, including the shoulders. The ruff should be immense and continue to a deep frill of hair around the neck between the front legs. The coat of the Exotic Shorthair is short, plush and dense.

In Persian type, the head should be a broad, round shape, massive, with great breadth of skull and a domed forehead. In profile, a straight line is seen from the forehead, nose and chin. The underlying bone structure is round, the cheeks full and prominent. There should be a sweet expression to

Persian Blue

the face. This is very important, as the cat should be pleasant to look at, never mean or frowning in appearance.

Jaws are broad and powerful with perfect tooth occlusion. The short nose should be as broad as it is long, with a definite break between the eyes. Some prefer a deep nose break and a turned up nose. Others prefer a break with the nose taking a slightly downward turn. As long as the standard does not specify which is correct, either is acceptable. Yet it must be remembered that the nose must fit in the straight line of the dome and chin, therefore the shorter, turned-up nose would best meet this requirement. The chin is strong, full, and well-developed, fitting into the round face. The neck should provide adequate support for the massive head and should be short, thick, well-muscled and powerful. The small ears are set wide apart and low on the head, always fitting into the rounded contour. The ear furnishings on the longhairs should be long and curved. The eyes are large, round, full and expressive and are set wide apart. The eye color should conform to the coat color, the deeper the better.

Persian Black and White / Blue and White

Introduction of the White Spotting Gene

The white spotting gene brought about a marriage between white and all the rest of the Persians' colors and patterns. This was not without great resistance from some breeders, who did not want anything to do with the white spotting gene and fought vigorously to prevent the "and whites" from gaining championship status, believing that the gene would ruin their bloodlines. Theirs was a lost cause and today, no one can doubt the beauty of these color combinations.

Variants

The presence in a Persian of chocolate, cinnamon, frost or fawn, colors associated with the Siamese, upsets some Persian breeders who severely frown upon a Persian with Siamese in its background. Many organizations do not recognize these as acceptable Persian colors; others list the chocolate and frost as Kashmirs, and give them an individual breed status.

Chocolate and frost Persians were recognized in TICA around 1980. There were not many of them. Their proud owners were dismayed when the cats did not go up in finals. They had overlooked one very important factor: color does not a cat make; type is more important. They had the unusual, a new Persian color, but they did not have good enough Persian type to win a final award. It takes years of breeding to produce the desired type in any breed.

Persian Black ♂ 0•11

Persian Head: round; broad; domed; snub nose; definite break; forehead, nose and chin in straight line; full cheeks. Ears: small; wide set. Eyes: large; round; wide set. Body: cobby. Coat: longhair.

Persian Blue Tortie ♀ 0·10

As the old saying goes, you build your barn, then you paint it. Also, chocolate is a glorious but miserable color to work with. It fades unevenly, it is either too dark or too light, and it can turn yellow.

Today, the so-called variants are the phenotype Persians from Persian parents having the pointed gene and are shown with the Persians in TICA regardless of color. Many are of excellent Persian type, and it would be impossible by looking at them to determine whether they have a Himalayan in their background. It would take a pedigree to prove they may not be full-colored cats in genotype.

Is it possible for two pointed Himalayans to produce a full-color Persian? Absolutely not. Is it possible for a Himalayan and a Persian to produce a Himalayan? Only if the Persian carries the recessive pointed allele. Is it possible for a Persian and a Persian to produce Himalayans? Absolutely, if both parents carry the recessive allele for pointing.

Persian Tortoiseshell and White ♀ 0·08

Red

The red Persian was reportedly developed in Great Britain early in this century. This is an extremely difficult color to work with, as the red displays a tabby pattern. The standard calls for solid red, sound to the roots; a virtual impossibility in the head area. In order to eliminate any tabby markings on the body, legs and tail, the cat would have to be an agouti tabby. The cat would also have to be golden or rufoused, which would increase coloring in the yellow band or the smeared granules of that band to a warmer, apricot color, the orange and apricot bands giving the visual effect of one solid-colored hair shaft. It would have to be bred for polygenes to enhance or deepen the "red" coloring. The hairs on the face will have to be long enough to disperse the "M" on the forehead.

Cream

The remarks concerning tabby and red also apply to cream. Careful breeding, using knowledge of genetics, is the way to produce the desired, solid-appearing color. Cream is extremely difficult to describe, just as it is difficult to match this color in yarn or to create it with watercolors. Many standards make no attempt to describe the color, except as a pale-toned cream, neither fawn nor red, pure and sound throughout without shading or rich tone. The very elusive good cream color should be a pale buff, never red or dark. If the cream has too much red tone it is referred to as a "hot cream," which is not desirable. Young cream adults will often appear to be shaded, having a lighter, ivory undercoat, much to the

Persian Tortoiseshell

Persian Blue Smoke ♂ 0•11

the terms for this group of colors, and geneticists cannot agree as to which alleles are responsible for the color changes. What is seen in these color variations, whether they are on American Shorthairs or Turkish Angoras, is an overlay of color on a lighter color. Such "tipping" is seen at its maximum effort in the Persian, due to the thick coat, long guard hairs and the abundance of down hairs. The ends of the

dismay of judges who will penalize for color or try to transfer these cats to the "shaded" division. This pseudo-shading will vanish with age, sometimes taking several years to go away and for the cream color to solidify. In the growth of the hair shaft, most colors will be darker toward the tips and lighter toward the body.

Tipped

Shaded! Tipped! Color variations! What alleles are involved and where are they? There is little agreement on

Persian Black Smoke ♂ 0•08

Persian Blue Tortie Smoke ♀ 0·08

hairs are pigmented with either eu-melanistic or phaeomelanistic colora-tion; the lower non-pigmented portion is "silvered" a silvery white. In the reds and creams, the lower portion may be more of an ivory white than a silvery white. Cats that are tipped but not sil-vered are called chinchilla or shaded goldens, as the undercolor is enhanced with the golden or rufousing gene.

Chinchilla silver Persians are breath-taking. They sparkle, shimmer and re-flect; when coupled with large, green eyes, the contrast is unbelievable. The Japanese have beautiful chinchilla,

Himalayan Black ♂ 0·06

Himalayan Tortoiseshell ♀ 0·06

shaded silver and golden Persians. There are not very many chinchilla or shaded silver breeders in the United States; only a few have achieved the perfect combination of beautiful shaded color and Persian type. The situation was so frustrating for some breeders that they petitioned, unsuccessfully, for acceptance of the chinchilla and shaded Persian as a separate breed.

The difficulty appears to be that if the silvers are bred to each other, green eyes are retained but type may be lost. If silver to solid is tried, the type comes back, but the eye color is lost. This does not apply to all silvers. There have been magnificent chinchilla silvers shown in North America over the past years.

The shaded black or the pewter is similar to the shaded silver except that the eye color is copper or orange and the undercoat is white, not a silvery white.

Cameo or Red Chinchilla

Equivalent to chinchilla silver is a "shell" or red chinchilla or "cameo." The coloring is almost beyond verbal description. It is like a thin layer of orange sherbet on top of vanilla ice cream, a two-toned, layered effect. Eye color is copper or orange.

Smokes

The smoke tortie gives another visual effect of black/red color tipping on a white undercolor. The smoke blue tortie is delicate in color. A black smoke appears to be solid black until the hair is parted to reveal a beautiful contrast of silvery white undercolor. Some believe that the smokes are non-agouti and not tabbies. This would depend on the definition of smoke. If smoke refers to the three-quarter pigmentation of the hair shaft, then any full color and pattern may be smoked. By traditional color terms, smoke refers to the tipping of the solids and torties; silver refers to tabbies (those with a pronounced, visible tabby pattern) and chinchilla or shaded silver refers to tipped silver tabbies with little or no visible tabby pattern.

Persian Shaded Silver

Persian Shaded Golden   ♂   1·08

Grooming

Persians have a very thick, woolly undercoat, causing the hair to be thick and plush, but this goes hand in hand with matting. They have to be combed and brushed constantly to keep the hair from matting, and they have to be bathed often. Large mats will form very quickly and often cannot be combed out but must be cut. The blues are especially guilty about matting up; some can go a few days without combing while others require daily care. Do not plan to own a Persian unless you have adequate time to give to grooming. Every judge should show a Persian at least once, to know what the exhibitor goes through to present an impeccably groomed animal.

Persian Shaded Silver / Shaded Golden

Exotic Shorthair Red Spotted Tabby ♂ 0•09

Exotic Shorthair Black ♀ 2•11

Exotic Shorthair Head: round; broad; domed; snub nose; definite break; full cheeks; forehead, nose and chin in straight line. Ears: small; wide set. Eyes: large; round; wide set. Body: cobby. Coat: short; dense.

Exotic Shorthair

The Exotic Shorthair is a man-made breed, the result of selective breeding programs to produce a Persian type without long hair. This attempt started in the United States in the 1960s and was greeted with screams of outrage from some Persian breeders. Ultimately, through perseverance, Exotic

Exotic Shorthair Tortoiseshell ♀ 0·09

Exotic Shorthair Blue
♂ 2·05

Shorthairs were recognized for championship competition and have delighted cat fanciers ever since.

To obtain the shorthair allele, another breed had to be crossed with the Persian; most Exotic Shorthair breeders selected the American Shorthair. Burmese and British Shorthairs were also used, but since 1968 these two breeds have not been allowed as outcrosses. Many early Exotics did not have good Persian type, but today's Exotics can have exquisite Persian type as well as the Persian's mellow disposition.

Exotic Shorthair breeders are very exacting about the length and texture of their cats' short, dense, plush coat. If the guard hairs are too long, the coat

Exotic Shorthair / Persian Blue Tortie

will drape down; this is not desirable. There should be an abundance of undercoat. Exotics have been called "Persians in pajamas," because unlike the Persian whose faults may be disguised under long hair, with the Exotic what you see is what you get. In TICA, the pointed and the parti-color point are two recently recognized color patterns. As of May 1989, in TICA, the Exotic is recognized in all colors and patterns, including the sepias and minks. The pointed Exotics are a delightful color pattern and have been referred to as "panda bears."

The cuddly Exotics share qualities of the Persian without requiring constant grooming, making them popular not only as show cats but as pets.

Exotic Shorthair
Blue and White ♀ 0•11

Exotic Shorthair
Black and White ♂ 3•07

Himalayan Head: round; broad; domed; snub nose; definite break; forehead, nose and chin in straight line; full cheeks. Ears: small; wide set. Eyes: large; round; wide set. Body: cobby. Coat: long. Pattern: pointed.

Himalayan

The idea of the Himalayan may be traced to a geneticist in Sweden in 1922, who set about to introduce the pointed allele into the Persian gene pool. Longhair whites were bred to Siamese. Whether this was successful is unknown, as records of the results are unavailable. In 1924 there were reports of pointed longhairs, called Malayan Persians, but these cats soon disappeared from the record.

The Himalayan as we know it was developed in the 1930s in Britain and in North America. The breedings in the United States combined Siamese with smoke, silver tabby and black Persians. These crosses produced several shorthaired kittens. Two of the kittens were mated to produce a longhaired black female, who was mated to her sire. This mating produced the first longhaired pointed kitten, named Debutante, born in the United States in 1935. It took five years to produce Debutante, who was very Siamese in type. The breeding experiments in the United States were done primarily to gain more knowledge of domestic feline genetics. Breeders in Britain were to work toward establishing a new breed.

It took years of hard work to produce the necessary three-generation pedigree. In 1955, Himalayans received a breed number and a standard; in 1957 they were granted championship status. By the 1960s all cat organizations recognized them as a separate breed; different colors and patterns, however, are accepted. In TICA, all pointed colors are recognized, including the parti-color points.

Himalayan Red Point ♂ 0·11

The early Himalayan did not resemble the Himalayan of today. There was no choice but to breed to Siamese to obtain the pointed allele; this brought the tendency to favor fine boning, straight profiles, larger ears, wedge-shaped heads, close-set eyes, longer bodies and a long narrow tail—all completely undesirable in the Persian. Obtaining and keeping blue eye color was another problem. It was thought that breeding to a Persian with weak eye color would improve the deep blue color so greatly desired. This proved untrue. To improve the eye color, the Himalayan should be taken to a Persian with the deepest eye color possible, such as a copper-eyed Persian.

The goal of Himalayan breeders to produce a pointed Persian, of all the man-made breeds, has been one of the most difficult to accomplish. For a time, only breeding Himalayan to Himalayan was allowed. As with the Siamese, breeders worked with solid points, always working for perfection of type. With each introduction of a color pattern, such as tortie or tabby, the Himalayan breeders were forced backward: in order to obtain the new pattern, they lost type. Breeders soon found that they had to breed back to the Persian to avoid losing Persian type. Today, the results of many years are evident in the show ring as a marvel and a source of pride. Himalayan breeders continue to work hard in their

Himalayan Red Point   ♂ 0·02

seldom run, jump or climb. They can have a surge of energy and suddenly romp like a kitten, but for the most part they are content with a very quiet life. Himalayans are so quiet that the females will not always give evidence of being in season by loud calling. They are well-suited for apartment or city life where less vocal cats are appreciated, and they are not as demanding as the foreign-typed cats. Most of them love being groomed. They are extremely easy to show and very rarely give the judge trouble, due to their gentle nature. These are the true nobles of cat fancy.

pursuit of the pointed Persian.

The silver lynx points might be explored as a wonderful addition. The silver should intensify the point color and lighten the body color. The silver and golden alleles should serve as color enhancers in the Himalayan, just as they have done in the Persians. Himalayans are now being produced with excellent Persian type while retaining the beautifully colored extremities and the blue eyes.

Himalayans are known for being calm and quiet, as little disturbs them, yet their curiosity is fully intact. They

Himalayan Cream Point
♂ 0·05

Himalayan Tortie Point   ♀ 4·01

Ragdoll

The blue-eyed, pointed, semi-longhaired Ragdoll is one of the largest and most docile of all the breeds. It loves being carried draped around its owner's shoulders, just like a limp ragdoll.

Origin

The exact origin of the Ragdoll is unknown. The breed may be only about twenty years old, and it is not known whether this is a man-made cat or a stroke of Nature. The early Ragdolls, so the story goes, were the result of kittens born to a white Persian who was injured in an automobile accident. Due to this accident, the kittens were supposedly free of pain or fear and were very docile. Most biologists would dispute this theory!

The genotype of the Ragdoll would have to include two alleles: the genes for pointing and for white spotting. If one of the parents was a white Persian, it would most probably be a dominant white with white spotting, carrying one gene for pointed. There is no information about the sire. He would have to be either a pointed cat or a cat carrying the pointed gene.

General Description and Judging

The Ragdoll is a semi-longhaired pointed cat of considerable size, with a very sweet and docile disposition. The ideal Ragdoll grows exceptionally large and heavy. Full development of color is not achieved until two years of age. Full weight and size are not achieved until the cat is at least four years of age.

The head is of medium length and is a broad, modified wedge with rounded contours, with a flat plane between the ears. The chin is well-developed. The nose profile shows a gentle stop. The medium-sized ears form a continuation of the modified wedge. The eyes are to be blue and are large and oval.

The cat should be firm with no fat except on the lower abdomen. The long body should be large and substantial, with a full, broad chest. The tail should be long. The legs are medium in length, with medium-heavy boning and musculature. The back legs are to be higher than the front legs. The feet are large, round, and tufted between the toes.

The semi-longhaired coat lies with the body but separates as the cat moves. It is longest around the neck, giving the appearance of a bib. It is shortest on the face and medium to long on the sides, stomach and on the hind legs where it is thick and feather-like.

Colors and Pattern

Ragdolls are shown in solid point and parti-color point (mitted and bi-color patterns only), and in seal chocolate, cinnamon, blue, frost and fawn colors.

The solid points have ears, mask, feet and tail of a darker color. The lighter body color is to be sound to the roots. In the mitted pattern, the legs (except for the feet), ears, mask and tail are a well-defined color. A white blaze (broken or evenly matched on each side) on the nose or between the eyes is accept-

Ragdoll Seal Point ♂ 4·07

Ragdoll Blue Parti-Color Point
♂ 0·08

Ragdoll Head: broad; modified wedge; slight stop. Ears: medium. Eyes: large; oval. Body: long; substantial. Coat: semi-long-hair. Pattern: Solid Point and Parti-color Point (mitted and bi-color).

able. The front feet are to have evenly matched white mittens (toes). The back feet are to be white, extending no higher than mid-thigh. The white must go around the hocks entirely. The body will have a white stripe which may vary in width. This stripe may extend from the bib to the underside (between the forelegs) or to the base of the tail.

In the bi-color pattern, the ears, mask and tail are defined in color. The mask is to have an inverted "V" which must be the same on each side and is not to extend beyond the outer opening of the eyes. The chest, stomach and all four legs are to be white. The color on the body may be a shade lighter than the points, with markings of white.

Temperament

Ragdolls are docile, gentle, quiet and easy to get along with. They enjoy human companionship and seem to have a "nothing bothers me" attitude toward life. They make sweet and endearing pets and are very easy to show, due to their gentle nature. Children and Ragdolls mix very well; the cats appear to love being carried around by children.

Ragdoll Seal Parti-Color Point ♂ 1·02

Russian Blue

With its silver-tipped blue hair, green eyes and thick double coat, the rare "Archangel Cat" from Russia is different from any other recognized breed. It may have been the ancestor of some of the present-day "blue" cats.

Origin

The Russian Blue may have originated in the area of the city of Archangel in northwestern Russia. Merchant sailors brought them to Europe in the mid-1800s. They have been known by many names: Archangel, Maltese, Foreign Blue and Spanish Blue. They were reportedly shown in the Crystal Palace in England as early as 1871 and were shown with other blue cats, not as a separate breed. In 1912 they were given separate breed status. They

Russian Blue ♀ 1·03

gained in popularity until World War II, when, like so many other cat breeds in Britain, they almost became extinct. They survived through the efforts of one English breeder.

The early Russian Blues had orange eye color and did not look like the contemporary breed in that they were cobby in body and rather round-headed. In the 1940s and 1950s Scandinavian breeders began crossing the Russian Blue with Siamese carrying the maltesing gene. Breeders in Britain began crossing the Russian Blue with blue point Siamese. With the introduction of Siamese genes into the limited Russian Blue gene pool, type and eye color changed. The Russians became longer in all aspects, and finer boned; eye color changed from orange to green.

General Description and Judging

The Russian Blue is an elegant cat. The foreign body type is not readily seen as it may be obscured by the dense, double coat. Preference is given to the lighter, silver-blue color. The hair shafts should be pale blue tipped with silver, so that each hair reflects the light, giving the coat a sparkling effect that dazzles the eye. Touching a Russian Blue feels like running a silk scarf through your hands.

The almost round green eyes are set wide apart. The large ears are placed wide apart and quite low on the sides of the head. The cat should have a sweet, smiling expression. The head is an angular, modified wedge consisting of seven flat planes. The first plane is from the top of the forehead to the bridge of the nose. The second is from the bridge to the end of the nose; the third is from the tip of the nose to the bottom of the chin. The fourth and fifth planes are formed by the skull on the side of the head, below each ear to the muzzle attachment. The sixth and seventh are from each side of the muzzle to the chin.

Russian Blue Head: modified wedge; flat planes. Ears: large; wide set. Eyes: large; almost round; green. Body: foreign. Coat: shorthair; double. Color: solid silver-blue.

Russian Blue ♂ 2•11

Russian Blue ♂ 0•05

Temperament

Gentle and shy, Russian Blues are easily startled and prefer delicate handling. Some of the Russian Blues of the 1960s had a bad disposition. Many judges would breathe a sigh of relief when the Russian judging was over, having escaped one more judging session without being eaten alive. But Russians imported from Sweden contributed a loving and sweet disposition, and today their descendants are a delight to keep. They are affectionate and loyal to their owners.

Scottish Fold/Longhaired Sco

With huge round eyes, deliberate, slow movements and folded-down ears, the owlish appearance of the Scottish Fold is unique among cats.

Scottish Fold Blue Tortie ♀ 0•11

Scottish Fold Blue Mackerel Tabby and White ♀ 0•06

tish Fold

occur. These could be gnarling of the feet, a condition resembling arthritis, or cartilage growth around the joints that would make it very difficult for the Fold to walk. Breeders have found that if the tail is short and stiff this may be evidence of stiffening in other parts of the cat's body. The exact cause of this condition is not known. If the hardening is caused by modifying genes, it may be possible to reduce their action or to eliminate them by selective breeding. Other breeders consider these concerns to be unfounded, and claim they have bred the homozygous dominants together without any adverse effects.

Choice of outcross is of course important for healthy kittens according to breeders who maintain that only Folds

Origin

This is a new breed that began as a spontaneous mutation discovered in 1961. A white kitten with folded-down ears was born on the McRae farm in Scotland. This cat, named Susie, was "discovered" by William Ross, a Scottish shepherd. The McRaes promised to alert Ross and his wife Mary if any more kittens with folded ears appeared. Two years later Susie had kittens, and two in the litter had folded ears. One was a male that was given away as a pet and the other, a white female named Snooks, was given to the

Rosses. Snooks in turn gave birth to a white male with folded ears, and the Scottish Fold breeding program was on its way.

The gene causing the folding of the ears was a non-lethal mutation, a single dominant gene (possibly an incomplete dominant). The responsible gene appears to manifest itself in the cartilage in the ears and may affect cartilage development elsewhere in the body. There is some controversy about breeding the Folds. Some breeders feel that if homozygous dominants are bred together, other abnormalities may

Scottish Fold Tortoiseshell and White ♀ 0·09

Scottish Fold Head: round; slight inward curve to short nose; prominent cheeks. Ears: medium; folded down. Eyes: large; round. Body: semi-cobby. Coat: short; dense.

Scottish Fold
Blue Mackerel Tabby ♂ 1·00

in the heterozygous genotype should be bred. The breed has been established by crosses to British Shorthairs and domestic cats in Scotland and England. In America the outcrosses are Exotic, American and British Shorthairs. The British Shorthair outcross produces a denser coat and rounder eyes.

Scottish Fold Red Mackerel Tabby and White

General Description and Judging

Kittens are born with straight ears; the folding does not begin until they are about two or three weeks of age. The overall impression of the Fold is roundness. The small to medium ears are set in a cap-like fashion on a rounded skull, and are folded forward and downward. The smaller, tightly folded ear is preferable to a loose fold and large ears. The large, round eyes are separated by a broad nose. Rounded, full cheeks and muzzle add to the desired full look. In profile, there is a slight stop.

The semi-cobby body is medium-sized, well-padded and even from shoulder to hips. The body and the medium to short legs are medium-boned with sturdy muscles. The tail is tapered and should be no shorter than two-thirds the length of the body and must be flexible. The longer tapering tail is preferred. The dense and resilient coat is short or semi-long.

Longhaired Scottish Fold

Early Fold breeders in Great Britain bred Susie and her descendants to British Shorthairs. Since the Persian, in Great Britain, is a legal outcross for the British Shorthair, the longhair gene was in the gene pool. Susie and her daughter Snooks both produced longhaired kittens, and longhaired Folds have appeared in litters with shorthaired Folds for many years.

TICA granted the Longhaired Scottish Fold championship status in May 1987. The longhairs should be judged using the shorthair standard, except for the coat length and texture. The dense, semi-longhaired coat should stand away from the body.

Temperament

Scottish Folds are very sweet, gentle, quiet cats. They make no demands on life, other than to be close to the people they love.

*Scottish Fold Brown
Classic Tabby and White*
♂ 1·05

*Longhaired Scottish Fold
Brown Classic Tabby* ♂ 0·06

Scottish Fold Longhair Head:
round; prominent cheeks. Ears:
medium; folded down. Eyes:
large; round. Body: semi-cobby.
Coat: semi-longhair, dense.

Siamese/Balinese/Oriental Sh

The lithe and graceful, long and lean Orientals, Siamese and Balinese are the prima donnas and ballet dancers of cat fancy.

General Description and Judging

These breeds are all described with the name Oriental: Oriental Shorthair; pointed Oriental Shorthair (Siamese); Oriental Longhair; and pointed Oriental Longhair (Balinese). The four breeds have the same type; they are separated only by variations in color, pattern and hair length.

They are beautiful and they know it. The Oriental type is characterized by large ears, a wedge-shaped head, a long neck, a long body and legs, and a long, whippy, pointed tail. To handle a Siamese or Oriental is likened to feeling a silk glove over an iron hand. These cats are fine-boned, delicate in appearance, long and elegant in every extreme while retaining firm, hard muscles. They should feel as hard as a rock, never emaciated or too thin.

Siamese Chocolate Point
♀ 1·08

from the center of the forehead to the tip of the nose and from the tip of the nose to the bottom of the chin. There should not be a whisker pinch; that is,

The wedge-shaped head, which ends in a fine muzzle, should fit into a long, triangular shape. In profile, a straight line without a dip or rise is seen

Siamese Seal Point ♀ 1·04

the line from the side of the chin to the base of the ears should be straight, with no indentation where the muzzle attaches to the skull. Large, broad-based ears extend and complete the triangular head as a continuation of the wedge and are angled slightly forward. The English ear set, wider apart and lower on the sides of the head, is preferred by some breeders and judges.

The medium-sized, almond-shaped eyes should be approximately one eye's width apart, with a slant toward the nose and the outer aperture in line with the center of the ear base. This combination of eye shape, size, placement and set gives the eyes a decidedly oriental look. If the forehead is too broad, the eyes will be too far apart and the cat will not have the desired look. The slender, graceful neck is carried to display length and adds to the elegance of the cat.

The long, tubular, narrow body is medium in size, with fine or slender boning and hard muscles. The legs are long with fine boning, the hind legs longer than the forelegs. The feet are oval, small and dainty. The tail is long, narrow at the base, tapering and whippy.

The Siamese and Balinese are pointed cats, while the Oriental Shorthair and Oriental Longhair are colored, patterned cats. The Siamese and the Oriental Shorthair should have short, close-lying coats; the coat looks as if it has been painted on with a high-gloss lacquer. The Balinese and Oriental Longhair should have semi-long coats; the hair on the tail is usually longer than the body hair.

Siamese

Origin

The Siamese cat is reported to have originated in Siam (Thailand). Old paintings show a cat with darker color on the ears, face, paws and tail.

Early Siamese in England and America bear little resemblance, apart from color, to the show Siamese of today. The early Siamese had short, stocky bodies, round eyes and short, round heads (present-day language refers to them as "apple heads"). The top show Siamese is now very extreme, long and pointed in every direction.

There were large classes of Siamese shown in the United States in the 1960s. The large Cat Fancier's Association show in Houston, Texas, quite often had as many as sixty-five to seventy Siamese. This is not true in the 1980s in the United States. Eight or ten Siamese are considered a large class; two or three is an average entry for most shows. What happened? Some believe that the Siamese breeders

Siamese Blue Point ♀ 2·03

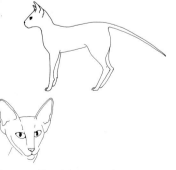

Siamese Head: long; wedge-shaped; straight lines. Ears: large. Eyes: medium; almond; slanted. Body: oriental. Coat: shorthair. Pattern: pointed.

Siamese Red Point ♂ 0•09

velop or mature before losing his show career to color. (The Orientals, on the other hand, are wonderful to show as kittens; they then go through the growing stage and may not be shown for months, returning when they are about eighteen months old and getting better and better each month.) For many people, it is too much to spend hundreds of dollars on a Siamese with a limited show life.

Temperament

The Siamese-Orientals are vocal; not only are they vocal, they are loud. A queen in season calls with an ear-splitting voice; a lonely stud cat will cry out for a mate twenty-four hours a day. Their calls may be heard for a very long distance. This makes it difficult, if not

were greedy in their desire to obtain that "certain look." In the 1960s and 1970s if the cat had that look it most probably had a cat named Fan Tee Cee in its background. Tee Cee was reportedly the Siamese that changed the whole concept of the Siamese. He abruptly appeared on the show scene in the early 1960s and blew every other Siamese clear out of the field. His head and body were very long; his eyes were almond-shaped; his coat was short. Some exhibitors, judges and breeders could not stand his extreme look, others longed for it. To have Tee Cee in their cats' pedigrees was good; a double-up of Tee Cee was even better. The risk is always high, in doubling up, of bringing two unwanted recessive genes together. And the more inbreeding, the more chances of offspring becoming smaller and smaller.

Siamese Chocolate Lynx Point ♂ 0•05

Another problem was that there were so many Siamese available that breeders could not sell their kittens, and prices were lowered to the point that a cattery could not support the breed. Additionally, the average show career of a Siamese is usually over by the time the cat is eighteen months old. As the cat ages, the body may darken; many judges will not award a Siamese if it has a dark body. The Siamese really never has a chance to de-

impossible, to keep these cats in a breeding status in a city. As loving as these cats are, their calling may not make them popular with the neighbors.

These most vocal of all the breeds will often carry on a running conversation with their owners. Some people adore this constant dialogue; others can't take it, preferring a more quiet breed. But these cats' genuine love of people brings an assurance of close companionship.

They are active, and their minds

*Siamese
Seal Lynx Point* ♀ 1•00

seem to be whirling with activity. If they do not have a playmate, they will create one out of anything. Height beckons a flight up or down; they delight in jumping and have been seen to leap five feet in any direction with ease. They are not outdoor cats. Most will make no effort to escape into the great unknown.

They usually like warm places and

relish sleeping on top of the television, computer, radiator, or anything that generates heat. A heating pad turned on low is deeply appreciated in cold weather. Not just fond of people, they need people to touch and for people to touch them. They demand attention and affection. They delight in riding on their owner's shoulders, lap sitting, or

sleeping with their owner. Most will sleep under the covers with their head on the pillow as close to you as possible.

Siamese and Orientals require little grooming. Rubbing them with your hand is enough to slick the coat down and remove any dead hairs; terry cloth washcloths or chamois skins produce a glistening coat. The Balinese and Oriental Longhairs require an occasional combing, but their hair does not mat.

These super-intelligent cats make wonderful pets if the owner can put up with constant companionship. These cats want to be with you every moment: if you walk, they walk beside you; if you sit, they are on your lap; when you eat, they love to be beside you; when you sleep, they will share your sleeping space. They will befriend you for life.

Genetics

The gene for pointed coloring is an allele of the albino series. Siamese kittens are born white. The gene causing the color restriction to the extremities, or points, of the cat allows the points to be pigmented and does not allow development of the same intensity on the body. The extremities are colder than the body; under the influence of the pointed allele, the areas which are of a lower temperature will produce the

Siamese Cream Lynx Point ♀ 1·04

Balinese Frost Point
♂ 1·08

Balinese Frost Lynx Point
♀ 0·11

The absolute purists go even further, believing seal and blue points are the only true Siamese. Is it possible to have a red or cream point, a tabby or a tortie point Siamese? There is considerable disagreement among the registering organizations; some accept these color patterns as Siamese and others refer to them as Colorpoint Shorthairs. Some believe that all of the offspring of a colorpoint, even if they are seal points, are colorpoints forever, with no exception. For these organizations a Siamese may only be bred to a Siamese.

The colorpoints were recognized in England in the 1960s. In TICA, the Siamese are recognized in all of the pointed colors and patterns except parti-color point.

Red Points

The red gene was introduced into the Siamese gene pool in the 1960s for a

greater amount of pigment. The kittens are warm at birth, and thus are white, having no dark pigmentation. As the extremities cool, pigment is developed in the points; since the body itself remains warm, complete pigmentation does not occur.

Siamese having a fever may produce

Balinese Blue Point
♀ 1·00

"fever hair" or white hair in their mask. If there is a bald spot on the body due to injury or hair loss, the hair that grows back may be dark and will remain so until more new hair comes in. If a bandage is placed over the injured spot, the hair growing back will be lighter. Also there is a tendency for the body to darken with age, due to poorer circulation.

Siamese Versus Colorpoint Siamese

Purists believe that the eumelanistic solid points are the only true Siamese.

number of reasons. Some breeders hoped to lighten the body color of their seal points by breeding to the red points (it didn't work), while others simply liked the color. The early red and cream points were heavily tabbied, which was not good, as the standard for the solid points did not allow any tabby markings. The genetics of

Balinese Seal Lynx Point
♀ 2·05

Balinese Head: long; wedge-shaped; straight lines. Ears: large. Eyes: medium; almond; slanted. Body: oriental. Coat: semi-longhair. Pattern: pointed.

phaeomelanin was understood by a minority of breeders at that time, and the tabby markings persisted for many years. Phaeomelanin allows the tabby pattern to be seen; all red or cream cats will display tabby pattern to some de-

gree. This includes the pointed cats. The agouti or aby tabby pattern is the only pattern to work with if the tabby pattern, barring and tail rings are not

reestablish the Oriental type, but they were working with the sex-linked orange gene and had to breed certain colors of a certain sex to obtain the desired color and sex in the offspring.

There are many shades of red: the cat may be seal red, chocolate red or cinnamon red; among the shades of creams, there are blue, frost or fawn creams (not to be confused with the maltesed torties). The red and cream points offer a lovely contrast between the red point color, white body and blue eyes.

the original gene pool; it was probably introduced through the American Shorthair. The Oriental body type would be lost for many generations in order to obtain phaeomelanin. First generation kittens would not be pointed if the red outcross was not carrying the recessive pointed gene. When kittens from such outcrosses were bred to Siamese, approximately half the offspring would be pointed.

The breeders now had more difficult times ahead. Not only did they have to

desired. Once this was understood, it was possible to have "clear" reds and creams. The "M" marking on the forehead, as well as other facial tabby markings, will be present to some degree. The undesirable barring, necklaces and tail rings, can, for the most part, be bred out.

Apparently phaeomelanin was not in

Balinese Chocolate Lynx Point
♂ 1·07

Balinese Blue Lynx Point
♀ 0·09

Oriental Shorthair Black
♂ 1·02

Tortie Points

One result of the introduction of the red gene into the Siamese gene pool was the production of tortie points. The resulting colors, instead of being black and red, were seal brown and a modified red, due to the action of the pointed alleles on black and red. The tortie point with the desired blaze is most striking: the nose has a line of demarcation down the center; one side is seal and the other is red. The chocolate or cinnamon and red has a beautiful warm color; the blue or frost and

Oriental Shorthair Head: long; wedge; straight lines. Ears: large. Eyes: medium; almond; slanted. Body: oriental. Coat: shorthair.

cream is of a subtle, soft coloration. One disadvantage that occurs in many tortie points is that the body color may tend to darken in the typical tortie patches of color as the cat grows older.

Lynx or Tabby Points

In the United States, the early lynx points were rather coarse, large cats, still influenced by the genes that

Oriental Shorthair White
♀ 0·09

brought in the tabby pattern. The breeders of the early lynx points spent many years breeding out heavy boning and round heads to produce a cat that could be judged according to the Siamese breed standard. Many of today's lynx points may be more impressive than their solid counterparts, being just as fine-boned, long-legged and extreme in type.

Balinese

Early Balinese cats were reported to be the product of Siamese-to-Siamese breeding. They were not a sudden mutation, but the result of pairing of recessive longhair genes. The most likely introduction of the longhair gene into the Siamese gene pool took place in England during the World Wars, when it was necessary for breeders to outcross in order to retain a part of their bloodlines. Turkish Angoras would

Oriental Shorthair Blue
♂ 1·01

Oriental Shorthair Cream Spotted Tabby ♀ 1·03

Oriental Shorthair Silver Mackerel Tabby
♀ 0·05

length. Some Balinese standards list the coat length as semi-long, but this does not reflect the coat on many Balinese today. Breeders have had to go back to the Siamese to retain the Siamese or Oriental type, and in doing so, the coat has become progressively shorter. The tail, which before was a nice plume, is now not very full, the hair perhaps measuring one to one-and-a-half inches long.

The Balinese is a lovely cat. The medium coat allows the eye to see the long lines of this marvelous creature. Perhaps the shorter coat was meant to be—but not too short!

have been likely candidates for out-crossing, as the type is similar. At first, breeders could do nothing with the longhaired kittens. They could not sell or show them; if entered in a show, the cats would be disqualified as Siamese because of their longer coat. Balinese were eventually accepted, and were granted championship status in the 1970s.

One problem of the Balinese breeders in the United States is loss of coat

Oriental Shorthair Frost
♀ 0·09

Oriental Shorthair

The Oriental Shorthair, the full-colored version of the Siamese, is a highly stylized, man-made breed, identical in type to the Siamese.

In England, the various colors produced from breeding Siamese to domestic shorthairs, Russian Blues and other cats were given unique color names and were granted breed status according to individual color and pattern; kittens from the same litter could be registered as different breeds, based on their color or pattern.

Some early Orientals were chocolate in color with green eyes. In 1958 in England the Governing Council of Cat Fanciers recognized these chocolate-colored cats as Chestnut Brown Foreign Shorthairs; in 1970 the GCCF reverted to an earlier name, Havanas. The offspring of Havanas imported into the United States were bred for different type, retaining only the original eye and body color (they are described separately in this book).

Another color version, what many consider the true Oriental, is the blue-eyed white Oriental. In 1977 this breed was granted championship status under the name Foreign White. They were obtained by breeding dominant white cats to Siamese. The white masking gene masks any color the cat may be carrying. (A further extension of masking is observed in the blue-eyed Siamese itself, in that the pointed gene eliminates the pigment in front of the eye; the true eye color of the Siamese would be copper, gold, hazel or green.) Because the dominant white gene was used, these cats were not deaf. Though the dominant white gene masks other colors and patterns, some kittens in a litter would be non-white. These colored Orientals are given color names, such as ebony for black, chestnut for chocolate, lavender for frost and caramel for fawn. These names have been retained and are used by some registering organizations.

Oriental Shorthair
Red Agouti Tabby
♂ 1•03

phenotypically and genotypically a pointed cat with blue eyes. But points and blue eyes do not a Siamese make. There are many other pointed allele breeds in TICA (Devon Rex, Cornish Rex, American Curl, Japanese Bobtail, Manx, Cymric, Sphynx); these breeds are not of Siamese type. The Siamese, regardless of its ancestry, must be of Siamese type in order to be accepted as a Siamese.

The attitude of some breeders is that the Siamese from Oriental parentage will produce stronger, healthier kittens, because the Siamese gene pool is constantly being enlarged, reducing the possibilities of doubling up on undesirable genes. Siamese produced from two Orientals are lovely; there should

Oriental Shorthair
Chocolate ♀ 0•09

The best blue-eyed white Orientals may be the ones masking chocolate points. The chocolate point Siamese may have a deep blue eye color and a rose aura in the eye, reflecting a deep, purple blue.

Controversy still rages concerning the Siamese produced from two Orientals or from an Oriental and a Siamese. Are they Siamese? Should they be shown with the Siamese? How should they be registered? The pointed allele is recessive to the sepia allele and the full color allele. The pointed cat is

Oriental Shorthair
Brown Spotted Tabby ♀ 0•06

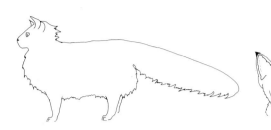

Oriental Longhair Head: long; wedge; straight lines. Ears: large. Eyes: medium; almond; slanted. Body: oriental. Coat: semi-longhair.

Oriental Longhair Black ♀ 0·04

be no visual difference between the kittens from a Siamese to Siamese, Siamese to Oriental Shorthair, or an Oriental Shorthair to Oriental Shorthair breeding.

Oriental Longhair

This recently recognized breed obtained championship status in TICA in the mid-1980s. The Oriental Longhair should also be of Oriental type, with the hair length of the Balinese and the color and patterns of the Oriental Shorthair. Breeders, like the Balinese breeders, must be diligent in order to retain type and coat length.

Oriental Longhair
Chocolate Spotted Tabby ♂ 0·06

Singapura

The native cat of Singapore. It is recognized in one pattern and color: seal sepia (sable) agouti tabby. The color is unique, a mixture of seal brown and oatmeal. This powerful cat is reportedly the smallest of the recognized breeds.

Origin

The Singapura traces its ancestry to cats picked up off the streets of Singapore and brought to the United States to be a part of a carefully controlled breeding program. The first Singapuras were imported to the United States in 1975. Hal and Tommy Meadows, in California, played an active role in working with these imports.

This is a rare breed in the United States and not many are seen in the show circle. There are about 250 Singapuras in the United States today, with over forty in the breeding program and a list of twenty-seven breeders. There is always a waiting list for kittens.

General Description and Judging

The Singapura is an alert, healthy, small- to medium-sized, muscular cat. The color is unique; this is the only recognized breed confined to the seal sepia (sable) agouti tabby color. The coloring consists of dark seal brown ticking on a warm, "old ivory" ground color, producing a delicate, almost sparkling effect. Muzzle, chin, chest and stomach are the color of unbleached muslin. Nose leather is pale to dark salmon. "Eyeliner," nose out-

Singapura Sable Agouti Tabby ♀ 1·04

Singapura Head: rounded; definite whisker break; slight stop permitted. Ears: large. Eyes: large; almond. Body: semi-cobby. Coat: shorthair. Pattern: agouti tabby. Color: sable (seal sepia).

Singapura Sable Agouti Tabby ♂ / ♀ 1·04

line, lips, whisker apertures, and the hair between the toes is dark brown. Footpads are brown. Salmon tones to the ears and nose bridge are preferred. The top of the head will appear browner as the shorter hairs have less ticking or banding. The head must be ticked or judges will withhold all awards.

The coat is very short in length, lies very close to the body, and is very silky in texture. The agouti ticked tabby pattern shows some barring only on the inner front legs and back knees.

The Singapura is smaller than the average cat. The semi-cobby body is me-dium in length, moderately stocky, firm and muscular. The moderate boning is heaviest at the shoulders. The tail tends to be slender, but it should not be extremely tapering or whippy. The legs are heavy-boned, muscled at the body and end in small, short, oval feet.

The extremely large, almost over-sized, almond-shaped eyes are an out-standing feature. They are held wide open and are set not less than an eye's width apart. The eye color may be ha-zel, green or yellow; no other color is al-lowed.

The face is relatively small. The head is round with a boxy muzzle on the rounded skull. In profile, there should be a very slight stop well below the eye level. A definite whisker break adds to the well-padded muzzle. The large ears are slightly pointed, wide at the base and medium in set. The neck is short and thick, but may be thinner in fe-males.

Temperament

Singapuras tend to be rather quiet and even-tempered. They are gentle cats and are quite loyal to their owners, but are curious enough to accept strangers willingly.

Sphynx

The "E.T." of cat fancy: the wrinkled cat; the hairless cat; the "hot water bottle" cat! Not completely hairless, the Sphynx is covered with a light down like the skin of a peach.

Sphynx Brown Classic Tabby and White
♂ 3·06

Origin

The Sphynx has been known as the New Mexican Hairless, or Canadian Hairless; in the 1970s it was given the name Sphynx. The Canadian Sphynx originated when a male hairless kitten was born in Canada in 1966 to a black and white house cat. This hairless male was bred back to his mother, resulting in a mixed litter of hairless and furry kittens. Other hairless cats have shown up in Paris, some of them reported to be the offspring of Siamese. The Sphynx was granted championship status in the early 1980s in TICA; it is not recognized by any other organization in the United States.

It is suspected that the gene for hairlessness (hr/hr) is recessive. One report of a Sphynx-to-Devon breeding producing all Sphynx kittens is intriguing. Is it possible that the hairless gene is dominant over the Devon Rex gene? Or is it possible that the Devon may carry the hairless gene as a recessive? It is also possible that there is an incomplete dominance resulting in Sphynx-Devon cats with "stubble" hair on the body and fur on the extremities.

General Description and Judging

Some people are repulsed by this cat, feeling it is the ugliest they have ever seen; others are charmed by it. It is so ugly it is beautiful. To hold a Sphynx is like holding a hot water bottle. Its temperature feels at least four degrees higher than that of other cats, though it really is no different.

The Sphynx is not a hairless cat; it is covered with a very short down that is almost invisible to the eye and undetectable to the touch. There may be short, tightly packed, soft hair on the points and a puff of hair on the tip of the tail, and there will be some hair on the testicles. Whiskers and eyebrows may be present, but are often broken or absent. The skin is wrinkled and should have the texture of suede. At first it was hoped that the Sphynx would be the answer for people who are allergic to cats. This is not the case, as the dander on the skin can produce allergic reactions. When the Sphynx sweats, with the sparseness of hair, normal follicular secretions may accumulate in the wrinkles; because of this the cat must be bathed often or wiped clean with a washcloth.

The Sphynx is hard and muscular; the medium-long body should be fine- or medium-boned but powerful, with a short, barrel-shaped chest. The front of the cat may be compared to a Boston bull terrier. The Sphynx should appear to be well-fed but not fat; this is not a delicate cat. The tail is long, whippy, tapering from body to tip (rat-tailed). The legs are long and slender, in balance with the body, but not fine-boned; they are firm and feel muscular. The hind legs are slightly longer than the forelegs. The paws are oval and dainty, with long, slender toes.

The head is slightly longer than it is wide, with prominent cheekbones and a definite whisker break. The profile has a distinct stop at the bridge of the nose. The very large ears are wide at the base and set upright. The large, round, lemon-shaped eyes slant to the base of the ears and are set slightly more than an eye's width apart and tend to be set back into the face. The muzzle is short. The neck is long and slender, giving an elegant appearance to the head.

Sphynx Head: modified wedge; distinct stop; prominent cheekbones. Ears: large; set upright. Eyes: large; lemon-shaped. Body: semi-foreign; full abdomen. Coat: short; fine down.

Sphynx Blue Classic Torbie ♀ 0·06

Temperament

Characteristics of the Sphynx include infinite patience and willingness to put up with almost anything. The Sphynx appears to be at great peace with the world, at ease with its surroundings, making a devoted pet and excellent show animal. You have to admire them. Even when they are sitting down, they hold their head up high, always showing refinement. The French standards describe them as "part monkey, part dog, part child and part cat."

Sphynx Cream ♂ 1·06

Tonkinese

The Tonkinese is the aqua-eyed, pointed beauty of cat fancy, a blending of Siamese and Burmese.

Origin

An American in the early 1930s brought home a cat acquired in Burma. Named Wong Mau, this cat is believed to have been a Tonkinese, not a Burmese. Tonkinese were not registered until the 1960s in Canada; championship status was first granted by the Canadian Cat Association. The early Tonkinese were sometimes called Golden Siamese, having Siamese pointing and the golden bronze-sepia pigmentation of the Burmese.

The Tonkinese belong to the albino series genetic system. The breed must carry one gene for pointing and one gene for Burmese or sepia coloration to produce the mink coloration. Tonkinese-to-Tonkinese breeding may produce one pointed kitten, one with Burmese coloring, and two Tonkinese. This allele allows the darker points, the slightly lighter body color, and a reduction of some of the pigmentation in the front of the eye, producing blue-green eye coloring.

General Description and Judging

The Tonkinese is unique in the cat world, a blending of the Siamese and Burmese in type and coloring. The cat is of moderate size and type, recreating the original intermediate type of its parent breeds, similar to the older version of the Siamese with the rounder head and shorter, somewhat heavier body.

The semi-foreign body, intermediate between the long, svelte Siamese and the cobby, compact Burmese, makes a strong, muscular cat of surprising weight for its size. The chest rounds gently in front, with the flanks level.

Tonkinese Frost Mink ♂ 0•10

Tonkinese Chocolate Mink
♀ 0·08

Boning is medium, neither heavy nor delicate, with well-developed muscles. There should be no sign of flabbiness or obesity; the abdomen should be taut. The tail is of medium length. The medium-long legs should be moderately slim, hind legs slightly longer than forelegs. The feet are oval in shape.

The head is a modified wedge with rounded contours, medium in size with a slight stop at or just below eye level. The muzzle should be blunt with a definite muzzle break. The head and ears should appear as an equilateral triangle. The high cheekbones are gently planed. The medium ears are pricked forward and are set as much on the

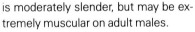

Tonkinese Head: modified wedge; rounded contours; slight stop; definite muzzle break. Ears: medium. Eyes: medium; peach pit-shaped. Body: semi-foreign. Coat: shorthair. Patterns: mink pointed sepia. Colors: eumelanin, solid.

side of the head as on the top, a continuation of the modified wedge. The oval, medium-sized eyes do not have an oriental slant but are angled on a line with the lower part of the ear. The neck is moderately slender, but may be extremely muscular on adult males.

The medium-short coat is soft, fine and silky, close-lying with a lustrous sheen, requiring little grooming. Tonkinese are currently recognized in the eumelanistic mink colors only: natural mink, chocolate mink, blue mink, fawn mink and frost mink. In some organizations, sepia and pointed (eumelanistic only) colors are accepted for championship status.

Temperament

The Tonkinese make healthy, beautiful, charming pets and show cats. They are quite active and love to run and jump, enjoying plenty of exercise. They are gregarious, outgoing and affectionate. The aqua eye coloring, the two-toned body with its soft, gently flowing contours, the blending of the Burmese and Siamese coloring, boning and personalities make the Tonkinese a very beautiful and endearing cat.

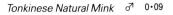

Tonkinese Natural Mink ♂ 0·09

Turkish Angora

An ancient breed originally from Angora (Ankara) in Turkey, the Turkish Angora has become a very rare breed. If two words could describe this beautiful longhaired cat it would be "flowing elegance."

Turkish Angora Head: modified wedge. Ears: large; set high. Eyes: large; almond. Body: foreign. Coat: semi-longhair.:

Origin

White Turkish Angoras were brought to France from Turkey long ago. They were bred to the sturdy, longhaired cats from Persia and Russia; the resulting kittens bore little resemblance to the long and lean Angora of today. They lost in popularity to the Persians, so that few were bred.

In the 1950s and 1960s, Angoras were brought to the United States directly from Turkey, and first received championship status in the 1970s. In Britain they were not known as Angoras until 1970, when breeders worked to recreate the long lines of the original Angora.

General Description and Judging

The Turkish Angora is a medium to small cat with a foreign-typed body, long, svelte and lithe, giving an impression of graceful, flowing motion on long, slender legs. The hind legs are longer, and the tail is a long plume. The coat is semi-longhaired with a silky, fine texture and little undercoat.

The medium-small head is a modified wedge, with a flat, long, medium-wide skull. The medium-long nose may be gently curved. The large, almond-shaped eyes are slanted toward the base of the ear. The large ears are set high on the head. The medium-long neck is slim and graceful.

Turkish Angora Blue
♀ 2·06

Temperament

The Turkish Angoras are elegant, truly the aristocrats of the semi-longs; regal, graceful and beautiful. They are usually gentle cats, easy to get along with and make colorful, affectionate, playful pets.

Turkish Angora Blue-eyed White
♀ 0·11

Turkish Van

A very old, rare breed originating in Turkey, the Van is famous for its pattern and for its love of water. The Turkish Van is also called the "swimming cat."

Origin

In 1955, two cat fanciers saw cats near Lake Van in Turkey that resembled the Turkish Angora, but instead of being solid white, they had deep, red markings on the face and tail. These cats not only could swim, they appeared to enjoy the water. Intrigued, the fanciers obtained a pair and returned with them to England. The offspring from these cats are the ancestors of today's Turkish Vans. In 1982, Barbara and Jack Reark imported Vans from France and the Netherlands to the United States, and bred and raised their kittens to have loving dispositions. Today, for the most part, they all have wonderful, loving dispositions, unlike the earlier Vans, who were notorious for their extreme dislike of being at cat shows and tearing into their owners, exhibitors or judges.

General Description and Judging

The Turkish Van is a powerful, semi-longhaired cat with distinctive markings. The base coat is white, with a white blaze between the markings on the head, and white ears. The body should be white and free of any color; the color markings should be restricted to around the ears and the tail, which is fully colored.

The short head forms a broad wedge with a slight stop in the nose between the eyes. The medium ears are large and held upright, and are spaced slightly wide apart. Different standards require the eye shape to be almond or almost round.

The long body is sturdy, broad and muscular, with wide shoulders. The medium-long legs are sturdy, with round, medium-sized feet; the hind legs higher than the front legs. The medium-long tail is a plume.

Temperament

This cat is incredibly strong, agile, quick, intelligent and striking in appearance, with an unusual affinity for being in water. The tail may be in constant motion, indicating the mood of the moment. Vans make devoted companions once their loyalty has been won.

Turkish Van Head: broad modified wedge; rounded contours. Ears: medium-large. Eyes: large; oval. Body: long; substantial. Coat: semi-longhair. Pattern: Van. Noted for red or cream tabby and white.

Turkish Van Red Tabby and White ♂ 0·07

New Breeds(Bengal/Snowsh

The new breeds are always exciting, as their committees must present something unique. It must be demonstrated that the basic type is different from any other recognized breed; color and pattern do not make a unique breed.

Bengal

The Bengal is the result of the hybridization of domestic tabbies and the Asian leopard cat. The first deliberate cross is believed to have taken place in 1963, but the breeding program initiated by Jean Mill was suspended and not reactivated until 1981 when Dr. Willard Centerwall entered into a partnership with Mill. The Bengal appeared on the show circuit in 1985.

The Asian leopard cat (now on the endangered species list) resembles a small ocelot, with longish large spots and stripes, and weighs about ten pounds. It is wild and cannot be tamed. Occasionally, a male leopard cat will accept a domestic cat and breed with her. The result of these breedings is the Bengal.

Breeders strive for the look of the first-generation Bengals, which resemble the leopard cat. The working standard features uniqueness: small rounded ears on a moderate-sized head; a wide nose; puffy, wide whisker pads; large, oval eyes. The nose is short with a prominent bridge and a gentle, inward curve from the bridge to the tip of the nose. The cat has a long, muscular, substantial body. The Bengals must retain the wild look of their forebears, and a coat, pattern and color that is unique to cat fancy. The spots are large and horizontally aligned; they do not follow the mackerel or classic pattern; some even have the beginnings of rosettes. The color is remark-

Bengal Leopard ♀ 0·08

able in that the eumelanin spots are on an orange ground color which is highly rufoused, almost red in color; the tail tip is black.

Temperament is of prime importance to this breed; these cats must be gentle, unchallenging and amenable to handing. Any sign of definite challenge will disqualify the cat from competition.

Snowshoe

The Snowshoe is a man-made breed, created by breeding a Siamese to a bi-color American Shorthair.

The parti-color pointed Snowshoe is a medium to large, shorthaired, semi-foreign type of cat that combines the heftiness of its American Shorthair ancestors and the length of its Siamese ancestors. It is very muscular, giving the impression of great power and agility yet having the look of a runner rather than a weightlifter. It is a well-balanced cat overall, with a very pleasant, people-loving nature. Average weight is eight to twelve pounds for males and six to ten pounds for females.

Snowshoe Seal Parti-Color Point
♂ 0·08

The unique combination of the pointed pattern with the white spotting gene and moderately long body type sets the Snowshoe apart from other breeds. When the white pattern is symmetrically marked against the darker points, the cat is most striking.

The head is a modified wedge with a two-planed profile that should fit into an equilateral triangular shape. The distance from the tip of the ear to the nose is the same as the distance from ear to ear. The ears are large, pointed, broad at the base and are set in a continuation of the modified wedge. The eyes are large, almond-shaped or walnut-shaped, with an eye's width between them; the outer corners are pointed toward the base of the ear. The nose is straight from the bridge to the tip; there may be a slight dip at the bridge. The cheekbones are high, but whisker pads are not pronounced. The neck narrows slightly from the head to the torso.

The body is rectangular, long but not overly extreme, well-muscled and boned, with a powerful, heavy build. There should be good heft to the body, so that the cat feels heavier than it looks. The females are not frail or dainty. The body should be flat without protruding shoulders. The long legs are muscular and firm, with back legs straight. The medium-sized feet are oval. The tail is thick at the base with a gradual taper to the tip. Tail length is equal to the body length from the base of the tail to the shoulders.

The Snowshoes are very sweet, gentle and loving cats.

Household Pets

The wonderful, often unique household pet comes in all colors and patterns according to the whim of Mother Nature.

Cats in this category have been discriminated against at cat shows for many years, being reduced to "fun rings" only. In early cat shows they were termed Alley Cats and, with their owners, were frowned upon by the owners of purebred animals. It has been a long struggle for owners to have their cats gain any recognition. They still have little or no recognition in some organizations.

In TICA, cats in the Household Pet category receive separate but equal treatment and enter the Household Pet show rings. These rings may be part of a regular show with licensed Household Pet judges or championship judges. All cats competing in this category must be altered.

A household pet standard provides guidelines, but, ultimately, beauty is in the eye of the beholder. The cats are a joy and a challenge to judge. Nature has often combined patterns or colors never seen in the championship cats. Many were found as abandoned kittens; some were from animal shelters or were strays who wandered into a home, capturing the heart of their new owner.

GLOSSARY OF TERMS

Aby Tabby or Agouti Tabby The least expression of the tabby pattern: agouti gene plus agouti gene. The legs and face may show tabby markings ("M" on forehead, frown lines, bars). The tail tip should be the darker color. Stripes or bars should be considered a fault, although specific breeds may permit light pencilings on the face, legs or tail. (Tᵃ/-)

Agouti Ticked or banded hairs; the agouti hairs are also found around tabby markings, making the tabby pattern visible. (A/-)

Allele One member of a pair or a series of genes that can occur at a particular locus on homologous chromosomes. (C/-, cᵇ/cᵇ)

Awn Hairs The coarser of two types of secondary hairs, having thickened tips (bristle tips).

Barring Tabby-striped markings.

Bi-color Pattern The cat has a colored back, tail and head with white on legs, feet, underside and lower flanks. A white blaze such as the inverted "V" pattern is often seen. Various markings of white and pigment may occur, but the cat is generally one-third to two-thirds white. (S/s)

Black Black color, with sound color from roots to tip of fur. (B/-, D/-)

Blaze A marking down the center of the forehead.

Blue Even gray-blue, lighter shades preferred. Paw pads and nose leather are slate gray. Individual breed standards allow variations on blue, such as Korat, Russian Blue, Chartreux. (B/-, d/d)

Break An indentation of the nose at about eye level or between the eyes.

Brindle (brindled, brindling) The scattered "wrong" colored hairs in the coat.

Brush A bushy, generally long tail.

Caliby A pattern of torbie and white, or patched tabby and white. (A/-, Xᴮ/Xᴿ, S/s)

Calico Tortoiseshell and white. (Xᴮ/Xᴿ, S/s)

Cameo A term used to describe the reds or creams and torties: shell cameo is a shaded red; smoke cameo is a red smoke; smoke cameo tortie is a smoke tortie.

Carrier A heterozygous individual carrying, for instance, a recessive gene. (A/a)

Cat Fancy The group of people interested in the domestic feline in general or in breeding or show activities. There are registering organizations in almost every country; they register cats and litters, maintain a pedigree data bank, provide judges, and issue show licenses and club charters. In some countries these duties are performed by individual clubs.

Champagne The term used to describe a sepia or mink chocolate color.

Chinchilla The least amount of tipping: coloring in which only the outermost tips of the hair are colored, the rest being silvery white.

Chinchilla or Shaded Golden Chinchilla golden is a gold to apricot undercolor, apricot preferred, with slight bronze or black tipping on the back, tail and legs. The chin is cream. The belly may be a lighter shade than the back. Rims of eyes, lips and nose to be outlined with black, and center of nose to be a brick red. Paw pads are slate gray to black. Tip of tail should be bronze to black as though dipped in ink. The whole effect to be a lighter golden color than the shaded golden. Shaded golden will have more color on the tip of the hair shaft.

Chocolate A rich shade of medium to dark chocolate brown, chestnut brown, or milk chocolate. (b/b)

Chromosomes The rodlike structures in the nucleus of a cell that control inherited characteristics. The physical site of nuclear genes, which are arranged in linear order. Each species has a characteristic number of chromosomes.

Cinnamon A medium, warm brown with red overtones, similar to the color of a stick of cinnamon, lighter than chocolate.

Classic Tabby A tabby pattern mainly of blotches and swirls highlighted by a "bull's-eye" on each side of the body. The cat should show good contrast between the pale ground color and the deep, heavy markings. The head is barred with frown marks extending between the ears and down the back of the neck to meet the "butterfly" on the shoulders, which divide the head lines from the spine lines. The spine lines are the wide, distinct stripes of darker marking color divided by stripes of the paler ground color running from the butterfly to the tail. The swirl on the side of the body should be an unbroken circle of ground color around a spot of marking color. Legs should be evenly barred with bracelets coming to meet the body markings; front of neck should have at least one complete necklace, and tail should be evenly marked with rings. Underside of the body should have rows of spots of dark marking color commonly called "vest buttons." (A/-, t^b/t^b)

Close-lying The coat lies very close to the skin.

Coat There are three main types of hair making up the normal coat: guard hairs; bristle or awn hairs; down or wool hairs.

Cobby A short, compact body with broad shoulders and rump. Usually with a short tail and a large, rounded head, as in the Persian, Himalayan, Exotic Shorthair or British Shorthair.

Cream A buff cream color, the paler the better. (d/d, X^R/X^R)

Curled Ears The ears curve up and back, away from the face. The distinctive feature of the American Curl.

Depth of Flank Determined by viewing the flank from top to bottom; the area between the rib cage and the thigh. The Manx/Cymric will have greater depth of flank; the Cornish Rex will have no depth of flank.

Dilute A paler version of a basic color, when the dense pigmentation is maltesed: black to blue, chocolate to frost, cinnamon to fawn, red to cream. Chocolate and cinnamon may be considered also as dilutions. (d/d)

Dilute Calico Any of the tortoiseshell colors maltesed; the eumelanistic and phaeomelanistic colors maltesed. Blue and cream; fawn and cream; frost and cream; blue, fawn or frost torties.

Domestic Type Heavier-boned, as in the American Shorthair, as opposed to the foreign type of the fine-boned Siamese.

Dominance The expression of one member of a pair of allelic genes in whole (complete dominance) or in part (incomplete dominance) over the other member. (A/a)

Dominant Describes the member of a pair of alleles that expresses itself in heterozygotes to the complete exclusion of the other member of the pair. The term also applies to the trait produced by a dominant gene. (A/a)

Dominant White White is the absence of color, the action of the dominant white gene. (W/-)

Double Coat A thick top coat of longer hairs over a thick undercoat. The awn hairs are the same length as the guard hairs. Russian Blues have a double coat.

Down Hairs Soft, crimped, secondary hairs.

Ear Furnishings Growth of hair extending horizontally from the ears.

Eumelanin The black- or brown-based melanin granules affecting pigmentation, hair, skin, eye colors; may be dense or maltesed. One of two kinds of melanin synthesis; the other is phaeomelanin. (B/-, b/b, b^l/b^l)

Fawn "Coffee and milk" color, a warm pinkish buff. (b^l/b^l, d/d)

Folded Ears The ears fold downward toward the face, due to a dominant gene affecting the cartilage. The distinctive feature of the Scottish Fold. (Fd/-)

Foreign Type Body type characterized by a long body with legs in proportion to body length; slim, fine boning; long, tapering tail; modified wedge or wedge-shaped head with large ears and oval or almond-shaped eyes. Abyssinian and Russian Blue are examples.

Frost Frost gray with pinkish tone; dove to light taupe gray; pinkish lavender. (b/b, d/d)

Gene The particular determiner of a hereditary trait; a particular segment of a DNA molecule, located in the chromosome. Genes are units of heredity which control growth, development and function of organisms.

Gene Pool The total of all genes in a species' population.

Genotype The genetic makeup or constitution of an individual, with reference to the traits under consideration.

Ghost Markings Faint tabby markings seen in some solid-colored cats, especially when young. These markings are not penalized in young kittens and are often allowed in young cats, according to individual breed standards.

Ground Color The area of color on the lower part of the hair shaft; also the agouti area between tabby markings.

Guard Hairs Longer, bristly hairs forming the outer coat.

Hairlessness Hairlessness is not absolute in the Sphynx breed; there is hair on the points; the body is covered with a light down. (hr/hr)

Harlequin One of the most extreme expressions of the white spotting gene. Color is limited to the extremities; several small patches of color are allowed. (S/S)

Heterozygous Having dissimilar genes received from each parent, of a given allelic pair or series, for a particular characteristic. (A/a)

Homozygous Having an identical pair of alleles for a particular characteristic. (A/A, a/a)

Inbreeding Breeding within the immediate family of closely related cats: parent to offspring or brother to sister; sometimes intentionally done to continue a unique trait. Inbreeding must be done with great caution and knowledge of genetics.

Incomplete Dominance or Partial Dominance The condition in heterozygotes in which the phenotype is intermediate between the two homozygotes. (L/L = shorthair, l/l = longhair; L/l could produce medium-long or medium-short hair.)

Inhibitor Gene This gene is believed to be responsible for the inhibition of color, and therefore responsible for tipping and silver. (I/-)

Kashmir A chocolate or frost Persian.

Lethal Gene A gene whose phenotypic effect is sufficiently drastic to kill the bearer. Death from different lethal genes may occur at any time, from fertilization of the egg to advanced age. Lethal genes may be dominant, incompletely dominant, or recessive.

Locket A small area of white or color that is different from the desired body color.

Lynx Point Tabby point pattern, such as in seal lynx point or blue lynx point. A pattern of tabby markings on the head, ears, tail and legs of a pointed cat. The body should be clear, not displaying a tabby pattern; if any pattern other than the agouti tabby is in the genotype, the body will show tabby pattern, especially as the cat ages. $(A/-, c^s/c^s, T^a/t^a)$

Lynx Tips or Tipping The extension of hairs from the tips of the ears. Lynx tips are desirable, for example, on the Maine Coon.

Mackerel Tabby Stripes run in a fishbone pattern, with no "bull's-eyes" or blotches. The sides of the mackerel tabby should be evenly barred with vertical unbroken lines of marking color similar to the rib bones of a

fish, hence the name. There are three distinct spine lines but they are very narrow and often meld into what looks like one wide stripe without fault. The head is barred with frown marks extending between the ears and down the back of the neck to meet the spine lines. Legs should be evenly barred with bracelets coming to meet the body markings; front of neck should be evenly marked with rings. Underside of the body should have rows of spots of the dark marking color commonly referred to as "vest buttons." (A/-, T/-)

Maltesing Also referred to as dilution. The clustering of pigment granules in the hair shaft. (d/d)

Mask Darker color covers the face, including whisker pads, and may be connected to the ears by tracings.

Masking or Epistasis The masking of the phenotypic effect of either or both members of one pair of alleles by a gene of a different pair. The masked gene is said to be hypostatic.

Melanin Pigment that gives color to the hair, skin, and eyes. Melanin produces eumelanin and phaeomelanin.

Mink The result of the action of the pointed and sepia genes on eumelanin or phaeomelanin. Seal (natural) mink, blue mink, chocolate (champagne) mink, cinnamon (honey) mink, frost (platinum) mink, fawn mink. Mink refers to "Tonkinese" colors. (c^b/c^s)

Mitted Pattern A predominantly colored cat with white limited to paws, back legs, belly, chest and chin in most specimens. The cat is about one-quarter white. (S/s)

Modified Wedge In the shape of the head, defined by individual breed standards, the straight lines of the V-shaped wedge are changed. Examples are: curved lines, gentle contours, no flat planes, the muzzle attachment flows gently into the skull and ears may be set slightly lower on the skull, as in the Abyssinian; or, an equilateral triangle, as in the Norwegian Forest Cat; or, a series of straight lines, including the forehead, the bridge to the end of the nose, the sides of the head to the muzzle, and the nose to the chin, as in the Russian Blue.

Modifiers Polygenes that change the effect of a major gene.

Multiple Alleles A series of three or more alternative alleles, any one of which may occur at a particular locus on a chromosome. The tabby system and the albino system are examples. (C/-, c^b/c^b, c^s/c^s, c^a/c^a, c/c)

Mutation A sudden change in genotype having no relation to the individual's ancestry.

Muzzle The projecting part of the head including jaws, chin, mouth and nose.

Muzzle Break Indentation where the muzzle is attached to the skull; whisker break.

Natural Mink Seal mink coloring.

Natural Protective Appearance Refers to the coat texture, water resistance, and hard protective coating of the hair shaft.

Necklace Tabby markings in the neck area.

Non-agouti The solid or self colors and tortie colors. The non-agouti gene prevents the formation of yellow banding. The hairs appear to be of one solid color. Red is inoperative on the non-agouti; non-agouti may work only in conjunction with eumelanin, so hairs containing phaeomelanin will always have agouti banding. (a/a)

Odd-eyed Having one blue eye and the other eye of another color, such as copper or orange.

Oriental Slant The cat's eyes are slanted toward the nose; the outer corner of the eye slants toward the center or just below the center of the ear; projection of the line from the lower eye corner would extend to the center of the ear base.

Oriental Type The head is long and triangular, the body is long and lean, the legs are long and fine, and the tail is long and whippy.

Parti-colors Coloring exhibiting the white spotting factor, regardless of the amount of

white (except for lockets) or the basic background color. Eye color should be the same as the corresponding coat color would be without piebald spotting, except that blue eyes and odd eyes are also accepted. Blue and odd eyes are more likely to occur in cats with greater amounts of white. Paw pads and nose leather may be pink or the color associated with the body color. A paw pad or portion of the nose may be one single color or mottled with both colors. (S/s)

Patching Clearly defined patches of color in the coat, as seen in torties, calicos and harlequins.

Pedigree The ancestral history of an individual; a chart showing such a history.

Phaeomelanin The red-, orange-, and yellow-based melanin granules affecting pigmentation, hair, skin and eye colors; sex-linked. One of two kinds of melanin synthesis; the other is eumelanin. (X^R/X^R or O)

Phenotype The appearance of an individual, based on genetic makeup.

Piebald White Spotting Prevents migration of pigment cells, preventing formation of pigment in areas on the cat, thus forming areas of white surrounding pigmented areas. (S/S or S/s)

Point Color Darker color limited to the extremities of the cat's body: the mask, ears, tail and feet.

Points The extremities of a cat's body: the mask, ears, tail and feet.

Polygenes Two or more different pairs of alleles, with a presumed cumulative effect, governing such quantitative traits as size and pigmentation. A small group of genes, when working together, can produce bodily characteristics.

Recessive The term applies to that member of a pair of genes which fails to express itself in the presence of its dominant allele. The term also applies to the trait produced by a recessive gene. Recessive genes express themselves ordinarily only in the homozygous state. (a/a)

Red On cats, a deep, clear, orange-red. In TICA, red and cream cats are shown phenotypically and registered genotypically. (X^R/X^R or X^R/y or O/-)

Reversed Ticking The outermost tip of banded hair is light instead of dark.

Rexed Appearing to be without guard hairs (guard hairs are present but are shortened due to the rex gene; the ends may be broken off); the hair is wavy. Two rex genes appear in cat fancy: the Cornish (r/r) and Devon (re/re).

Roman Nose There is a bump or arch to the nose; the nostrils are set low. The Birman has a Roman nose.

Roman Profile The forehead to the tip of the nose has a downward curve, as in the Cornish Rex.

Rosettes A variation of the tabby pattern whereby rosettes instead of spots are formed. The rosette pattern was seen on the Bristol Cat and is on some Bengals.

Ruddy The black agouti color in the Abyssinian or Somali is often referred to as ruddy. Orange-brown (burnt sienna), ticked with two or three bands of either black or dark brown, the extreme outer tip to be the darkest with orange-brown to the skin. Outer parts of the body covered by shorter hair are to have at least one band of ticking.

Rufous May be a polygene or the result of the action of a group of polygenes. The rufous factor changes the drab beige yellow band of the wild tabby to a brilliant apricot; it changes drab orange to a brilliant, rich red. The Ruddy Abyssinian is a rufoused black agouti tabby.

Sable Dark brown color; seal brown, seal sepia. (B/-, c^b/c^b, D/-)

Seal The seal brown, dark brown color found at the points of pointed, sepia or mink colors. (B/-, c^s/c^s, D/-); (B/-, c^b/c^b, D/-); (B/-, c^b/c^s, D/-)

Semi-cobby A variation of the cobby body type; not short like the Manx, not long like the Siamese. The British Shorthair and

American Shorthair are examples.

Semi-foreign A variation of the foreign body type, with long lines, medium boning, modified wedge-shaped head. The Havana and Egyptian Mau are examples.

Sepia A color resulting from the action of recessive genes on eumelanin or phaeomelanin. The term used to describe Burmese colors. Variations are sable (seal) sepia, blue sepia, chocolate (champagne) sepia and frost (platinum) sepia. May also be seen in cinnamon sepia, fawn sepia, red sepia and cream sepia. (c^b/c^b)

Sepia Agouti Tabby Seal brown, dark brown or sable brown ticking on a warm ivory ground color. The Singapura is a seal sepia (sable) agouti tabby. (A/-, B/-, c^b/c^b, D/-)

Shaded Coloring in which the tips of the hairs are colored, the rest being white or pale, the tipping being intermediate between chinchilla and smoke. Also referred to as the Shaded Division which would include chinchilla, shaded and smoke.

Shading Gradual variation in coat color, usually from the back to the belly.

Silver Ground color or undercolor has been silvered. The term applies to chinchilla or shaded silver, and silver tabby. The silver gene eliminates all yellow. Examples are silver tabbies and silver torbies.

Silver Lynx Point Silver tabby markings are restricted to the points; markings are darker than non-silvered lynx point. All yellow is eliminated; the body is almost white. The cat may be tabby or torbie.

Smoke The cat should appear to be of solid or tortie color until the hair is parted to reveal the pale or white undercolor. The hair shaft will have a large amount of color (three quarters of the hair shaft colored) on a smaller amount of pale or white ground color.

Smoke Colors The basic description is based on black smoke: the cat should appear jet black with a silvery white undercolor. Except for the silvery white frill and ear tufts on longhairs, the undercolor of the head, face, legs, back, sides and tail do not show until the coat is parted. The belly and underside of the tail may appear gray, shading down to silvery white.

Solid Point The result of the action of the pointed gene on the solid and eumelanistic and phaeomelanistic colors. Color is restricted to the points. The body will be several shades lighter than the points. Variations include seal point, chocolate point, cinnamon point, frost point, fawn point, red point and cream point. (a/a, c^s/c^s)

Sorrel Aby Cinnamon agouti tabby. A warm sorrel ticked with cinnamon brown. The tail is tipped with cinnamon brown. Paw pads are pink with cinnamon brown between the toes, extending slightly beyond the paws. In some organizations this color is called red but it is not a true red. (A/-, b^l/b^l, C/-, D/-, $T^a/-$)

Spotted Tabby The cat is marked by spots of a darker color, most prominent on the sides of the body. The spots may vary in size and shape, but preference is given to round, evenly distributed spots. A dorsal stripe runs the length of the body to the tip of the tail. The stripe is ideally composed of spots. The marking of the face and forehead should have typical tabby markings; the underside of the body should have "vest buttons." Legs and tail are barred. The pattern may be caused by a separate gene, modifiers or incomplete dominance of the tabby alleles.

Standard The term applies to a breed or color/pattern standard. Each recognized breed has a standard of perfection; this is usually set by a breed committee and verified by the breed section. The standard is made for the ultimate in "perfection," but it is probable that no cat will ever completely measure up to this standard.

Stop A change in direction: the short incline between the forepart of the skull and the muzzle, or, a concave curve occurring in the nose at or just below eye level; may be very slight or pronounced.

Tabby Tabby pattern is made up of two factors, the tabby pattern and the agouti (ticked) area between areas of the pattern.

Tabby patterns include ticked tabby, mackerel tabby, spotted tabby, and the classic tabby. Cats having non-domestic genes may have a rosette pattern.

Ticked Three or four separate bands of color on each hair shaft, as on the Abyssinian.

Ticked Tabby Ticking of the body hair with various shades of the marking color and ground color, the outer tipping being the darkest, the undercoat being of the ground color. The body may exhibit a barely perceptible fine pattern, resulting in a delicate, tweed effect, but distinct stripes, spots or blotches will be considered a fault. The tail, legs and face will have tabby pencilings. Necklace tracings are also seen in a well-marked specimen. (T^a/-)

Tipping Having colored ends on the hairs, with a different color on the lower portion of the hair shaft. The degree of tipping can determine whether a cat is classified as a chinchilla, shaded or smoke.

Torbie Usually a female cat: a tortoiseshell turned tabby, in which the black patches are tabbied forming a continuous pattern with the red patches. To determine if a cat is a tortie or a torbie: in the tortie the eumelanistic patches will be solid; in the torbie the eumelanistic patches will be tabbied. Also called patched tabby or tabby tortie. (A/-, X^B/X^R, [T/-])

Torbie Point Eumelanistic and phaeomelanistic patches of tabby markings are restricted to the points. The body will be several shades lighter than the points. Usually shown with the lynx points. (A/-, c^s/c^s, X^B/X^R, [T/-])

Tortie See **Tortoiseshell**

Tortie Point Body color is the same as the corresponding eumelanistic color point; the shading, if any, is in the same tone as the points. Body shading on the tortie point will be mottled. Point color will be a mottling of the corresponding eumelanistic and phaeomelanistic colors. A blaze is desirable. (c^s/c^s, X^B/X^R, T/-)

Tortoiseshell A mosaic of eumelanin and phaeomelanin patches. The colors may be maltesed to produce the blue tortie, frost tortie or fawn tortie. The amounts of eumelanistic and phaeomelanistic pigment are randomly determined during embryological development. An evenly patched cat with good delineation between the colors and a distinct streak (blaze) of the phaeomelanistic color on the nose is to be preferred. (X^B/X^R)

Tuck Up A curved spine creates the drawing in of the flank, as in a greyhound dog or the Cornish Rex cat; the opposite of depth of flank.

Type Conformation; the general form and structure of the body; different standards apply to different breeds.

Undercoat A true undercoat consists of the woolly or down hairs, under the longer guard hairs.

Undercolor The part of the hair shaft closest to the skin; in a smoke, the unpigmented portion of the hair shaft; in tabbies, the ground color.

Van Pattern Considered the most extreme expression of the white spotting gene. Color is restricted to the head and tail. One or two small body patches may be allowed. (S/S)

Wedge Referring to head shape as viewed from top/front: created by straight lines from the outer ear bases along the sides of the muzzle, without a break in the jaw line at the whiskers. The skull is to be flat and the straight nose a continuation of the forehead.

Whippy Referring to the tail: long, slender, tapering.

White White is usually listed as a solid color; it is not a true color but the absence of color, the outcome of the action of the dominant white gene alone or with the white spotting gene. Kittens and young adults may display a spot of color on top of the head, showing the masked color or pattern. This spot usually disappears at about eighteen months of age. (W/-)

Postscript

Time passes quickly: ten years have passed since I began to photograph cats. At home and abroad, the cat has been a remarkable photographic subject for me. I don't know how many times I've snapped the shutter, but the more I take photographs, the more the cat reveals its different charms, and I don't know where creativity stops and the cat takes over.

This book was planned for a long time, but it was difficult to find the opportunity to bring it into being. One day, Gloria told me there would be a big cat show in New York, and that I could photograph the cats there. I thought this would be a "now or never" chance to do the book. So, taking advantage of the opportunity, I traveled in the United States and Canada as well as in Japan, to see many cat shows and to meet cat breeders. It took me three years to complete the work; I took over 6,000 photographs of 500 cats. In the course of this work I met many breeders, who willingly let me photograph the lively cats of which they were so proud. I don't know how to thank enough these friends that I met thanks to the cats.

When I photographed at the cat show in New York, I was unaware of the crowd that gathered behind me. Someone called my technique "action photography." I would release the shutter while playing with the cat. To take photographs, my spirit and the cat's must be as one. If I were to ask someone else to make the cat play, I wouldn't understand the cat. That wouldn't work. Moreover, the cat would not strike the pose I'm looking for. For the cat to "pose" the way I want, I have to play with it myself. This was possible thanks to the camera, a Zenza-Bronica, which is adapted for use with one hand.

I hope that this book, intended to help the reader better understand the different breeds of cats, also reveals my abiding affection for cats.

Tetsu Yamazaki

With the collaboration of: The Garden Cat Club, Compadres Cat Club, Aby's Unlimited Cat Club, Klondike Cat Club, Excelsior Cat Association, Silvergate Cat Club, Southern California Cat Club, Tokyo Cat Club, Friendly Cat Club

Cameras: Zenza-Bronica SQ, 50mm, 80mm, 100mm, macro 110mm, Minolta X-1m Xd, 35mm, 50mm, macro 100mm
Film: Fuji 100D, Kodak 64